The Death of Napoleon

THE DEATH OF
NAPOLEON

SIMON LEYS

TRANSLATED BY

PATRICIA CLANCY

AND THE AUTHOR

Farrar, Straus and Giroux

NEW YORK

Library of Congress Cataloging-in-Publication Data
Leys, Simon.
*[*Mort de Napoléon. English*]*
The death of Napoleon / Simon Leys: translated by
Patricia Clancy and the author.
Translation of: La mort de Napoléon.
1. Napoleon I, Emperor of the French, 1769–1821—Fiction.
I. Title.
PQ2672.E99M6713   1991   843'.914—dc20   92-5122   CIP

FOR HANFANG

CONTENTS

What a pity to see a mind as great as Napoleon's devoted to trivial things such as empires, historic events, the thundering of cannons and of men; he believed in glory, in posterity, in Caesar; nations in turmoil and other trifles absorbed all his attention . . . How could he fail to see that what really mattered was something else entirely?

PAUL VALÉRY,
Mauvaises Pensées et Autres

The Death of Napoleon

I · A SUNRISE

ON THE ATLANTIC

AS HE BORE a vague resemblance to the Emperor, the sailors on board the *Hermann-Augustus Stoeffer* had nicknamed him Napoleon. And so, for convenience, that is what we shall call him.

Besides, he *was* Napoleon.

How the Emperor's escape from St. Helena eventually succeeded during the last stage of an extraordinarily ingenious plot is a story that has already been narrated elsewhere (see "The Prisoner of St. Helena" in *Fireside Stories*, June/July 1904). Suffice it to recall here the main outline of the stratagem: a humble and loyal sergeant who, in the past, had often served as a double of the Emperor was dropped on a beach of St. Helena one moonless night; simultaneously, Napoleon boarded a Portuguese seal-hunting lugger that had been chartered for this daring venture.

For the English jailers (as well as for the rest of the world) the next day was very much like any other day. Napoleon got up at the usual time, drank his customary *chocolat*, played (and cheated) at patience, and took his constitutional according to daily routine. Except for a tiny handful of devoted servants who were involved in the conspiracy, no one knew that these various activities were being performed by a double, and that the genuine Napoleon was sailing on the sealer that was to bring him a few weeks later to the island of Tristan da Cunha—a desolate rock, uninhabited except for a few penguins and other wretched natives whose description we shall spare the reader.

From Tristan da Cunha, he was given a berth on a crayfish schooner bound for Cape Town. At no stage of his journey was anything left to his initiative; every move had been minutely planned for him, and each time he was notified of it at the last moment, by a series of anonymous agents, themselves mere cogs that fitted blindly into a huge, mysterious machine. This second leg of the journey had been long and rough. He was traveling under the name of Eugène Lenormand; at the time, however, his assumed identity had little practical use: the crew of the schooner was made up of Norwegians who would never have considered speaking to him. This attitude did not reflect any ill will on their part—they were no more talkative among themselves—the fact is, after years of seafaring, these Scandinavian mutes had lost all aptitude for social intercourse. As a result, the resemblance—somewhat vague yet still discernible—which the newcomer presented to the hero who had shaken Europe and the world was not likely to provoke any embarrassing curiosity. And anyway, the only crowned head that was faintly familiar to the crew was that of a Danish king whose lithographic portrait was yellowing on the bulkhead in the forecastle.

Now, however, on the third and last leg of his journey, the situation had entirely changed. On board the *Hermann-Augustus Stoeffer*—the brig that was at last carrying him back to

France—the sailors were a fairly sophisticated collection of cosmopolitan scoundrels. They were not entirely devoid of *culture générale*: what is more, the boatswain was a Frenchman who had served on the Egyptian expedition and persisted in professing his Bonapartist religion. Yet, of all the crew, he would have been the most reluctant to acknowledge that there could be the slightest resemblance between his god and the new cabin hand (for it was in this capacity that Napoleon appeared on the roll).

It all began with a cheeky remark from the ship's boy.

One morning, as the boy had to carry astern the officers' breakfast trays, he called out to the cabin hand to come and help him. As the latter remained lost in his perpetual daydreams, the boy, who was observant and not without wit, finally shouted, "Ahoy! Napoleon!"

The effect far exceeded his expectations. The man leaped to his feet as if lashed with a whip. For a fraction of a second, his eyes lit up with the fearsome intensity of a wild animal caught in a trap. Although the boy was still young, life at sea and the rough company of the crew had already endowed him with a fair dose of cynicism; therefore, Eugène's brief metamorphosis did not overly impress him—he merely noted what appeared to be a fairly efficient method of bringing the cabin hand back to earth. As, in his daily chores, he frequently needed the other's assistance, he found the use of this new nickname very expedient.

The rest of the crew, continually hearing "Napoleon!" here, "Napoleon!" there, eventually ratified the vague resemblance there might have been between the cabin hand and the prisoner of St. Helena; thus, for everyone in the forecastle, he became Napoleon from then on.

The boatswain alone found the joke to be in very poor taste. That any form of association could be established between his idol and this ugly little man, with his potbelly and knotty knees, was sacrilege to him. It must also be said that Napoleon had aged considerably over the last few years; he had lost most of his hair and, to protect his head from the cold sea wind, had taken to wearing a woolen cap which his landlady on Tristan da Cunha had knitted for him in a mixture of gaudy colors. This comfortable but slightly ridiculous hat added the last touch to a silhouette the very sight of which was enough to irritate the boatswain.

The latter's exasperation was further exacerbated by the seeds of irritation repeatedly sown by the supercargo—an insolent young man, the son of a Birmingham solicitor, who had been banished to the high seas, having impregnated a parson's daughter. This odious Englishman, knowing the boatswain's devotion to the Bonapartist cause, took a perverse delight in addressing the wretched cabin hand with mock courtesy as "Monsieur de Buonaparte" whenever the boatswain was within earshot.

These indirect insults to his idol filled the boatswain with a rage which he usually vented upon the unfortunate Eugène. There were plenty of opportunities, for the cabin hand, being no good at anything, was obliged to do everything—there was no mindless, humiliating, or dirty task that did not eventually fall on his shoulders. Even the ship's boy had the cheek to unload some of his duties onto him.

Naturally, he was denied the essential dignity of the topmen, who, during their watches, could escape from the suffocating heat below decks, and, in the swaying of the spars and billowing whiteness of the sails, became like weightless giants, brothers of the seabirds in the wind. His physical debility chained him to the deck. Yet, what did it matter to him if he was a mere insect in the eyes of those aloft? He rarely looked up, even absentmindedly, in their direction. He endured his abject state with complete stoicism, making no attempt to evade his present condition. He was beyond all humiliation: his real self existed elsewhere, in a cold lucid dream flying to meet the future, toward France and empires still to come!

As everyone knows, sailors are a rough lot, but not mean-spirited. They tolerated him, paying as little attention to him as to the parrot of the cook Nigger-Nicholas. As long as he did as he was told, they had no quarrel with him. In actual fact, although they did not feel the slightest respect for him, something prevented them from bullying him. Was it his aloofness, his obstinate silence that created a certain distance, or his plump white hands, like a bishop's, that gave him a mysterious dignity? Perhaps they simply took pity on his physical weakness and his prodigious ineptitude in performing any sort of manual work.

The only creature to show him genuine consideration was Nigger-Nicholas. Not that this meant very much, as Nigger-Nicholas called everyone "Boss," even his own parrot.

No one knew exactly how old Nigger-Nicholas was. His appearance was quite loathsome. He was tall, but a good half century spent bending over stoves in low-ceilinged galleys had broken him up into several angular segments, like a half-folded pocket rule. Without really being fat, his body swelled out arbitrarily in places, giving him the shape of a semi-deflated balloon. His face was split by a huge gaping mouth; in this grotto, as black and dirty as the maw of his stove, there emerged one or two teeth, like slimy rocks protruding at low tide. The ruined state of his teeth made his speech, already bizarre, all the harder to understand, endowing his rare utterances with a kind of oracular force—as befits a black cook on a sailing ship who, to be true to type, must naturally have a smattering of occult sciences.

Napoleon paid no attention to the boatswain's hostility or the supercargo's sarcasm, and he ignored the brutish indifference of the sailors as well as the impertinence of the ship's boy. But he was equally unaware of the favors which Nigger-Nicholas regularly bestowed on him, and which inspired a certain amount of envy all round. As the cook can dispense a number of much-sought-after privileges—a juicy piece of crackling here, a pig's trotter there, a spot close to the stove for drying socks, a drop of hot coffee before going out on the dogwatch, etc.—he is always surrounded by a crowd of sycophants seeking his favors. Napoleon benefited from these various acts of kindness without doing a thing to earn them. He accepted them as his due, and most of the time did not even appear to notice them. The strange thing is that, far from discouraging Nigger-Nicholas, this very indifference seemed to increase his solicitude.

Every evening, crushed by the fatigue of the day's work, Napoleon would escape for a moment from the stuffy atmosphere of the forecastle and lean against the bulwark in the bows to watch the first stars come out. The softness of the tropical azure giving way slowly to the velvet of night, and the glittering of the lonely stars which seem so close to us when they begin to shine in the dusk, left him perfectly cold. He came and stood there purely for the sake of his health; he merely wished to refresh his body, relax his muscles, clear his lungs, and make sure of a good night's sleep.

If he cared so little for the magnificence of tropical sunsets, it was not because he was naturally insensitive to romantic grand operas. On the contrary! Yet, ever since the momentous night of his escape from St. Helena, he had decided to protect himself behind an impenetrable shell of indifference. At this stage of his uncertain journey "Napoleon" could be nothing more than a shipboard nickname, a grotesque joke of the forecastle.

At that very moment, it was an obscure army sergeant who was cast in the role of the wounded eagle, of the solitary prisoner, of the tragic exile, while the true Emperor existed only as a vision of the future. Between the persona he had shed, and the one he had not yet created, he was no one. For a time, Eugène would have to fill this blank interval with his mediocre existence; he had no right to a destiny of his own; at most he could be granted inglorious little misfortunes and a few petty pleasures.

Thus, he had to deny himself the intoxicating splendors of these sunsets for as long as he remained cut off from his true self, cast off from his own fate, left hanging in this halfway void, forgotten, between sea and sky, in the dull emptiness of this slow boat, among coarse sailors.

During this time in limbo, and until the day when Napoleon's sun would rise again, he had to survive by relying upon wretched Eugène's purely physical existence.

Only the slenderest thread was leading him back toward the hypothetical dawn of his future. So far, at every stage of his journey, a new, unknown messenger had emerged from the shadows to show him the route to follow.

For the time being, all he knew were the instructions that had been given to him at the last port of call: when the *Hermann-Augustus Stoeffer* arrived in Bordeaux, he should look on the wharf for a man with a mustache, wearing a gray top hat, sitting on a barrel, holding a furled umbrella in one hand and a copy of the *Financial Herald* in the other. This new contact would guide him to the huge secret organization that had been prepared to propel him back into power, and which needed only one spark of his genius to be set in motion.

He still had no idea how this organization worked, and none of his successive guides had been able to enlighten him on the subject; in fact, the fundamental rule of this amazing plot was to observe such absolute secrecy that the conspirators themselves did not know the very object of their association. Although the membership could already be counted in tens of thousands, no two members knew each other. Under such conditions, they naturally had no way of learning that the author of this gigantic scheme—an obscure young mathematician— had already departed this world two years earlier, carried off by brain fever! However, the complex mechanism that his brilliant mind had designed was so perfect, and every detail had been planned with such precision, that the wheels kept blindly turning day after day, month after month, without being affected in the slightest by the disappearance of their anonymous creator.

IN SPITE OF his firm resolve to keep Eugène strictly confined within the limits of his temporary role, there was one occasion when Napoleon's vigilance was caught off guard. The incident seemed trifling, but it was to leave a scar that was deeper than he probably realized at the time.

The *Hermann-Augustus Stoeffer* had crossed the Tropic a few days earlier and had now entered the zone where the trade winds were pushing her along steadily. With all her canvas up, the brig was sailing beautifully, heeling under a strong warm breeze which blew with such regularity that the crew hardly ever had to brace the yards. The watches were leisurely; it was as if the boat had made a pact with wind and sea, and had taken charge of the whole operation, leaving the sailors with little to do. And so the journey continued, night and day, sailing home on wings in this state of blessed truce with the elements.

One night, Eugène was awoken by a strong

hand shaking his shoulder. Still sleepy, in the dim light of the hurricane lamp that burned night and day in the forecastle, he made out the grinning features of Nigger-Nicholas, who was leaning over him. The cook, in a state of happy excitement, signaled him to get up and follow him right away.

Eugène would have preferred to go back to sleep. What on earth did this boisterous brute want with him in the middle of the night? But he had learned to be docile, and he would have meekly taken orders from the ship's boy himself. He tumbled out of his hammock, and still half-asleep, he staggered after Nigger-Nicholas to the ladder leading to the hatchway.

In the pale rectangle of sky outlined by the half-open hatch, he could see that, contrary to what he had first thought, night was almost over.

He climbed the ladder and stepped out onto the deck.

Nigger-Nicholas, who was waiting there for him, was literally dancing with delight. With the triumphant expression of an artist unveiling his masterpiece, and a wide sweeping gesture that took in the whole stretch of the horizon,

16

he showed him the dawn breaking over the ocean.

It was indeed an extraordinary sight.

The sky was divided between night and dawn—blue-black from the west to the zenith, pearl-white in the east—and was completely filled with the most fantastic cloud architecture one could possibly imagine. The night breeze had erected huge unfinished palaces, colonnades, towers, and glaciers, and then had abandoned this heavenly chaos in solemn stillness, to be a pedestal for the dawn. The highest crest of a windblown cumulus was already brushed with yellow, the first beam of daylight against the roof of fading night, whereas the lower regions of the clouds were still sunk in darkness, where one could vaguely make out deep gorges, shadowy peaks, rows of cliffs and blue chasms, nocturnal snowfields, and wide expanses of purple lava. The entire sky was caught in an interrupted surge of energy, frozen in motionless chaos. Above the smooth, translucent sea, everything was in a state of suspense, waiting for the sun.

Nigger-Nicholas, who was eagerly watching for the cabin hand's reaction, was not disappointed. Under the spell of that extravagant splendor, so unexpectedly presented to him, Napoleon was momentarily made one with Eugène, reconciled with himself by the impact of an ecstasy that obliterated both his dream of glory and his present humiliating condition.

Nigger-Nicholas was usually quite indifferent to sunrises. However, he felt very pleased with the success of his initiative, and above all, he was proud of his own perspicacity. He had been able to pick out Napoleon from the common sailors, for whom he had nothing but contempt; from the beginning, he had guessed that this was a different breed of man—almost his equal. And now his diagnosis had been fully confirmed: the cabin hand had obviously not been brought up on the same diet of lard and moldy biscuit as those ignorant sailors.

Delighted with his own sagacity, Nigger-Nicholas did not even wait till the end of the show. He went down into the galley to prepare the breakfast coffee.

The sun had set all the clouds ablaze with light. As the smell of coffee rose from the galley, the morning watch came on deck; with

18

great splashing of water and banging of buckets, the sailors began to swab the decks.

. . . The flamboyant mysteries of dawn had faded into the banality of plain day. The sky, which had earlier dominated everything with its overwhelming grandeur, was once more pale and distant, occupying its usual place in one half of the scenery, the other being filled by the monotonous sea, which sullenly rocked the *Hermann-Augustus Stoeffer*. The clouds which, by the end of the night, had climbed to the top of the sky had now scattered. The brightly painted giants of the dawn had shrunk and almost disappeared; all that remained of them were little white puffs straggling across the line of the horizon like grazing sheep.

The sky was clear; the breeze had died down. The *Hermann-Augustus Stoeffer* rolled heavily on the oily swell. A slack halyard drummed obstinately against the mast.

The heat began to rise. The new day had already grown stale: it had turned into an ordinary day at sea, blue and flat like any other.

Napoleon was carrying the breakfast tray to the officers' mess room. He suddenly felt weak. He had been wounded by the dawn and his burden seemed so heavy. Nigger-Nicholas's complicity had breached his defenses.

He wanted to be free of his debt to the cook. While polishing the brass in the captain's cabin, he stole two cigars, intending to present them to Nigger-Nicholas. But he immediately felt ashamed of his action. Had he already sunk so low, he who used to grant licenses for entire tobacco shops with one stroke of the pen?

II · WATERLOO REVISITED

ON A COLD SPRING MORNING, out at sea off Bordeaux, a small lugger came alongside, bringing a message from the shipowners to the captain of the *Hermann-Augustus Stoeffer*.

The news quickly spread among the crew: the brig was to bypass Bordeaux and sail directly to Antwerp. The sailors, who were looking forward to going ashore, were disappointed at the thought that their voyage was going to last at least another week.

As for Napoleon, he was positively thunderstruck. Just when he was finally about to reach port, a mundane decision made by some vulgar shopkeeper, based on the price of molasses or indigo, suddenly barred his way. However, he soon regained his composure. The invisible hand that had unfailingly guided him to this point would surely be able to ward off this unexpected blow. New arrangements were certainly being made at this very moment, he thought, to ensure that the connection would be reestablished in Antwerp.

Alas! He was still unaware of the full extent of his misfortune!

A nasty nor'easter blew continuously during the last leg of the journey, forcing the brig to beat all the way. The weather was cold, all hands were constantly on deck, and the sailors were exhausted and soaked to the skin.

The *Hermann-Augustus Stoeffer*, which was a mediocre sailer to windward, took no less than ten days to reach the mouth of the river Scheldt, and for Napoleon these ten days proved more grueling than the whole of the ten months that had elapsed since his escape. Too long under pressure, his physical resistance suddenly gave way. His old stomach pains started up again, and for more than forty-eight hours he was unable to take any solid food.

The mouth of the river was marked by flat

mudbanks whose blurry lines were barely visible on the horizon. The featureless landscape was drowned in intermittent rain squalls. The brig had to sail, now close to one bank, then to the other, following the invisible course of the main channel. Its meanders were known only to the pilot—a red-haired native who wore corduroy and wooden clogs like a farmer.

All through the months, Napoleon had waited with such fervent longing for this moment when he would finally see land again. His heart sank in disbelief as he stared at the gloomy banks, shrouded in gray, which bore no resemblance to anything he had imagined in his dreams of returning to France. Approaching this foreign shore, he felt as though he was beginning a new exile.

As the brig continued farther inland toward the port, the river became progressively narrower. One could now see the banks in more detail: muddy farms whose black thatch showed above the dikes, a red-brick church, forlorn windmills. This low, sodden countryside looked like some shapeless Patagonia lying in the desolation of an antipodean wasteland.

Napoleon's consternation increased as he

watched the landscape slowly unfolding. Over-whelming fatigue paralyzed his limbs. He felt old, sick, and lonely. Taking advantage of this immense weariness, the voice of cowardly, cynical Eugène whispered inside him, tempting him with words of abdication and surrender.

The brig came alongside the wharf.

His senses dulled by rain and exhaustion, he did not even recognize the Napoleon Basin, which he had personally inaugurated ten years earlier. In the meantime, it had been renamed Wilhelm Basin, in honor of some king of Holland.

It took him no time at all to pack his bag. He left on board most of his possessions—oilskins, sea boots, etc.—which would be of no further use and would only add weight to his luggage.

He went ashore. Incapable of rational thought, all he could do was to repeat to himself the last instructions he had received ten months earlier. He knew them by heart, as they had been the mainstay of his hopes all through the long days at sea.

The wharf was deserted. No sign of a top hat. Not even a barrel.

He waited for a long time, pacing up and down.

From time to time, a lone passerby would walk along the quay. He gave a start each time anyone appeared. Standing in a conspicuous spot, he would anxiously scrutinize the face of every newcomer in the hope of discovering some secret sign of identification. But the dock-worker, hurrying home, did not even look up as he approached. And the ragged old woman picking out peelings from between the cobble-stones with her hook was so absorbed by her work that she did not pay him the slightest attention.

A rain squall drove him to take shelter in an open shed. The cold was beginning to go right through him. He stood there, lost and dejected, like a kite cut adrift from its line and dumped by the wind at the back of some vacant lot, hidden from view.

He had finally lost the only thread that had guided him back since his escape! A single grain of sand had derailed that wonderfully precise

25

machine, which would still continue to turn, but would turn blindly and to no purpose. Napoleon was left to his own resources; from now on, he would have to struggle alone, groping in the dark to find his own way back toward the glorious dawn of his future.

BEFORE MAKING any new plans, he had to find shelter for the next few days.

As he did not have the energy to walk very far, he entered the first private hotel he came to, in a narrow street that wound around the foot of the cathedral.

In the hallway, there were aspidistras in highly polished brass pots; a red carpet led to the stairs. These signs of bourgeois prosperity made him apprehensive about the bill, but it was too late to retreat.

His room, crowded with elephantine furniture adorned with antimacassars and lace, was small and smelled of wax polish. Once alone, he began to count his money. All he had was his seaman's pay. It was a modest sum, but it should be enough to meet the expenses of the journey to Paris. However, before setting out

26

on his final and decisive venture, he needed first of all to regain his strength. At the risk of making serious inroads into his capital, he decided to rest for a day or two in these quiet surroundings.

For the next twenty-four hours, he scarcely left his room. At this crucial turning point in his destiny, he needed time to reflect as much as he needed rest.

Yet it was almost impossible for him to collect his thoughts. There was some important festival going on in the town. What were they celebrating? He intended to find out about it from the maid who cleaned his room, but then he forgot to ask her. What did it matter anyway?

Breaking away from the processions that must have been marching down the boulevards, small groups of people wearing grotesque masks sometimes wandered into the narrow street, dancing and laughing down below his window. The blare of brass bands could be heard in gusts now and then.

Then, on Sunday afternoon, there was a carillon concert in the cathedral. The bell tower, whose massive walls plunged the entire little street into perpetual gloom, blocked the horizon of Napoleon's window like a dark cliff. For three whole hours, his room was taken over by the bells. It was terrifying. The big bells boomed and roared mercilessly, while the smaller bells spilled out tinkling cascades of sounds. His room, the boardinghouse, the entire street shook under the pounding of those enormous ringing hammers. Deafened and stupefied, Napoleon sat on his bed, staring dumbly at the hydrangeas on the wallpaper, while his skull seemed to disintegrate under this barrage of bronze.

Finally, that same evening, members of an Artists and Writers Association came for a meal of mussels in the banqueting room on the first floor. But by then the drinking songs no longer had any effect on Napoleon: he had at last slipped into a dreamless sleep.

ON THE MORNING of the second day, the weather cleared up. It was still quite cold, but the sky was full of blue patches through which the sun splashed pools of light against walls and roofs.

Napoleon was feeling better already. He paid his bill and boarded the coach for Brussels.

Once on the road, in spite of the jolting of the old carriage, he felt a surge of new energy at the very thought that he was traveling south and that each turn of the wheels was taking him a little closer to Paris. Between brief showers, there were long intervals of sunshine during which the countryside looked green and bright. The gentle lines of the fields, woods, and meadows had a soothing effect on his mind, pushing away the nightmarish memories of his journey; the funereal river at his arrival and the long limbo at sea, where his very soul was almost destroyed, seemed now remote and unreal. With their bells tinkling gaily, the four horses pulled the coach along at a brisk pace. The wheels thundered over the round cobblestones, while the passengers watched leaning rows of poplars whisk past.

Once in Brussels, feeling thirsty, he went to the Hôtel de la Poste for something to drink before making any decision about the next stage

of his journey. While paying for his coffee—
a sour-tasting beverage which unfortunately
was already reawakening his old ulcer—he
suddenly saw a brightly colored notice stuck
on the mirror behind the counter. It was written
in English, being obviously intended for British
tourists. Although Napoleon knew nothing of
that language, the meaning was not hard to
guess.

VISIT WATERLOO
& THE BATTLEFIELD!
Special coaches. Interesting prices for groups!
Take your inscription here!

"What can I do for you, sir?" asked the
woman behind the counter, putting down a tan-
kard that she had just washed. "Ah yes, Waterloo. Certainly, sir. We have a group booking
for tomorrow morning. The coach leaves from
the front of the hotel at a quarter past nine. If
you would like to join it, we can still book you
a seat. One florin sixty-five return, drinks not
included; but for a supplement of forty cents,
you can have lunch at the Caillou Inn, and a
qualified guide will take you around the bat-

30

tlefield . . . Shall I make a booking for you, sir? Would you like to leave a deposit?"

Napoleon dropped a half-florin on the counter.

The woman tried to book him for the guided tour and the lunch, but he firmly refused to be talked into extra expense. His stay in Brussels and the excursion to Waterloo were an unexpected outlay that had to be offset by a stricter economy. The next morning, all he took with him were two bread rolls wrapped in newspaper. These modest provisions should last him for the day.

The coach left at the appointed time. It was packed, for, besides Napoleon, there were six Englishmen and six English ladies. They set off at a good pace on the road to Charleroi. Although it was only April, the weather was exceptionally warm and sunny.

The ladies went into raptures over picturesque features of the scenery, while the gentlemen observed the countryside with an air of smug satisfaction, as though they owned it.

After an hour, the coachman pointed with his whip to a greenish onion dome that capped a brick church and announced: "Waterloo!"

whereupon a ripple of excitement spread among the tourists.

Napoleon was the only one who did not share this lively mood. The sweetness of this pleasant morning in the country made him slightly queasy. He was overcome by a strange feeling of anxiety.

THE PARTY MAKES a first stop at the village of Waterloo-l'Eglise, to visit the Brasserie de l'Empereur, a large farm that has been turned into an open-air café with a dance floor. On the rough, freshly whitewashed front wall hangs a notice:

THE EMPEROR SPENT THE NIGHT HERE
BEFORE THE BATTLE.
VISIT NAPOLEON'S BEDROOM

Underneath, in smaller letters, is a timetable and a list of admission prices, with reductions for "Groups, Children in the Company of Adults, Servicemen in Uniform & Others."

The twelve English tourists rush into the

building and up the stairs to see the historic bedroom.

Napoleon does not follow them. Suddenly he feels faint. The vague malaise that has been upon him all morning at the sight of that smiling countryside where the shadow of a soft gray cloud occasionally caresses the hills abruptly gives way to an overwhelming certainty: he realizes with horror that HE HAS NEVER BEEN IN THIS PLACE BEFORE!

The English tourists are on their way down.

Recovering his composure, he, too, enters the farm, crosses the paved hallway, and climbs the narrow staircase leading to the first floor.

Napoleon's bedroom is sparsely furnished with the basic items: iron bed, plain wooden table, wooden chair with straw seat, jug and basin on a painted chest of drawers. The paper on the walls has garlands of mauvish flowers.

He takes the whole room in at a glance.

The horses are stamping impatiently down below. The coachman is counting his passengers, ready to set off again.

He cannot stay any longer. He stares desperately at the unfamiliar room, seeking vainly for some clue; his eyes slide over a blank surface, making no contact. He suddenly feels dizzy, he can hardly stand. He stumbles downstairs, his legs shaking, and finds himself back in the coach, which sets off immediately. On to Mont-Saint-Jean!

"Mont-Saint-Jean! Everyone out, please!" The coachman reminds his passengers to be back by six o'clock for the return journey.

The return? Napoleon has no intention of ever going back to Brussels. There is no looking back, his mind is made up. If he can steadfastly confront a second Waterloo—all the more daunting a task on such a beautiful spring day—if he can emerge victorious from this strange trial he has so recklessly set himself, he will immediately make his way to Paris by the old Charleroi road; he will allow nothing to delay him. In his sudden eagerness to rush forward and to engage in the last decisive struggle, he superbly forgets that he has not yet paid his bill at the hotel in Brussels.

Turning his back on the ludicrous charabanc that has brought him to this crucial encounter with himself, he walks down the other street in the village—the one which the twelve English tourists have not taken. This time, he does not bat an eyelid as he passes by the Café de la Grande Armée, which also boasts a tricolor signboard:

VISIT NAPOLEON'S BEDROOM!
THE EMPEROR SLEPT HERE
THE NIGHT BEFORE THE BATTLE!
Special prices for families and school parties!
Taste our famous local specialty, cherry beer!
Customers' own food may be eaten on the premises!

A girl is standing on the doorstep. She is shy and sweet, and asks him in her rather slow Walloon drawl, "Don't you want to see Napoleon's bedroom?" There are obviously not many visitors at this time of the year. But the lies of all the museums in the world cannot affect him anymore. He keeps walking, irresistibly drawn on by the softly rising curve of meadows and fields at the other end of the village. From there, the unchanging circle of the plain comes into view, and it is there that he has an appointment with his own destiny!

However, he will not be there alone.

On the side of the road stands a makeshift little hut which also bears a notice announcing:

EDMOND, VETERAN OF NAPOLEON'S
OLD GUARD, SURVIVOR OF THE LAST
BATTLE SQUARE. GUIDED TOURS OF
THE BATTLEFIELD.
BY APPOINTMENT.

The owner of the premises, with his unkempt beard, squats on the doorstep, waiting for appointments.

As Napoleon passes in front of him, he gets up—or more precisely, he gathers together the remains of his person, for it then becomes apparent that one leg is missing, one arm is withered and twisted like a dead twig, and he has lost half an ear and perhaps an eye, unless he is just cross-eyed. He hauls himself up on a crutch, clumsily mended with string, and tries to follow. Taking pity on his efforts, Napoleon slows down to allow this heroic but gruesome physical wreck to follow with less difficulty.

And thus they climb the hill—the pale little man and the broken-down scarecrow—an odd couple born of the same dream of glory. As they make their progress across the plowed fields, flocks of partridges take flight in front of them. A cuckoo is singing in the wood nearby.

When they reach the lookout point that dominates the whole plain, Edmond the Veteran automatically launches into his set piece without waiting to be asked. He has trotted it out so often that he knows his monologue by heart, and points out the historical landmarks in the surrounding countryside—La Papelotte, the Caillou farm, the Holy Hedge, the Sunken Lane—without even bothering to look at them, so well does he know where to find these permanent buoys in the ocean of fields and meadows. On the plain, the only movement—if you can call it that—comes from groups of sleepy cows. A plow drawn by three horses that move so slowly they seem to be standing still knits new black furrows, one after the other, into the gray and yellow surface of a fallow field.

Although the words of Edmond the Veteran betray the effects of constant repetition to tourists, behind the hackneyed expressions and affected rhetoric, the attentive listener can detect an authentic ring in the evocation of the epic battle that this simple man must have lived through, body and soul. As if hypnotized by the deathly pale little man, the guide finds himself departing imperceptibly from his prepared speech. Closing his eyes, he abandons himself to the flow of his memories, and begins to relive the whole ordeal, as it happened, from dawn to dusk. "It was raining on that day, it was pissing down . . ." And in spite of the peaceful sunshine and the pure song of an invisible lark piercing higher and higher into the blue sky, like a medium in a trance he summons up and brings to life the real spirit of the plain. Before Napoleon's very eyes, the false decor of pastoral calm, with its fields and cows and plow on the horizon, parts like a naïvely painted country scene on a theater curtain, revealing the somber truth that is always there, hidden behind the veil of appearances.

. . . In a murky twilight, under a low sky, men, horses, and cannon are once more bogged down in the mud. Across the sodden fields comes the loud rumble of regiments on the move, while the muffled boom of cannon can be heard in the distance. The men have been marching all night to meet their fate, weary as beasts of burden; here and there in the grass, a few are already dead, their eyes wide open with astonishment.

Yet when did this vision, which at first seemed so overwhelmingly true in every detail, suddenly become confused and begin to fall apart? Napoleon again experiences the same dizziness that he had felt in the unfamiliar bedroom. Edmond the Veteran foams at the mouth and screams and whirls around on his crutch like one possessed, as he goes through all the torments of that incredible day. Under this hail of words, Napoleon is horrified to discover the image of ANOTHER Waterloo, which is more and more difficult to reconcile with his own memory and sense of logic. He can no longer find a single landmark on the plain; even as he stares at it, the scene becomes weirdly distorted. Edmond the Veteran's incantation is drawing him into a whirlwind where his reason falters and is about to be swallowed up. He struggles to break free; with one final effort, he suddenly resists and interrupts his relentless guide: "No, no! It's not the grenadiers who are holding Belle-Alliance, it's the dragoons! . . ."

Edmond the Veteran stops short. In the sudden silence, the song of the lark fills the air again.

Now there are only two men walking in the sun, deep in an interminable and petty argument about the positions of the Grand Army. Neither will give in. Edmond the Veteran with a sly sideways glance has the last word: "I should know. I was there."

Napoleon changes the subject. "Have you ever seen the Emperor?" he asks point-blank.

Mollified, but with a hint of mockery, Edmond the Veteran stares at him, narrowing his crafty eye. "Why, he was as close to me as you are! . . ."

Then he starts off again, suddenly quite aggressive, as if he wanted to express his complete contempt for this puny tourist who, a few minutes ago, had had the impudence to contradict him. "The Emperor was young and handsome like a god. You have no idea." He raises his eyes, contemplating a heavenly vision. Against the sky, between the clouds, he can see him once again on his white horse, reviewing the front line of his troops, while the long row of busbies and rifles begins to waver and sway like a wheatfield under the wind, and a thousand voices, hoarse with fever and smoke, roar in unison, "Long live the Emperor!"

But he quickly looks down again; his mobile features become almost repulsive as he adds, scarcely moving his lips, "Between you and me, Napoleon was a vampire. It was our blood that kept him going. You should have seen him in the evenings after a battle. The toughest veterans of the Guard were crying from sheer exhaustion, but there he was, passing among us, fresh as a daisy; he would look at the dead and wounded, wading through the blood. That's where his energy came from. Take me, for instance—he's gouged out my eye and bitten off my leg. Look, I can see that you are a man of the world. You, you're not one of those tourists full of warm tea and gherkin sandwiches. Perhaps you've been a soldier, too? Well then, I'll show you my war wounds! I don't show them to just anyone, you know! There are always English tourists who would gladly pay extra, just to have a look, but they haven't got a hope! It's none of their business! But between the two of us, it's quite different. You and I, we speak the same language—no need to stand on ceremony."

As he finishes his patter, he begins to unwrap his stump from the empty trouser leg, which was furled around itself and secured with a large rusty safety pin. He performs the unswaddling like a professional, with quick, precise gestures. The whole routine has something ritualistic and vaguely obscene about it. But at the end of it, when he raises his head, he realizes that his customer has already left some time ago and is heading downhill toward the village. "Hey, friend! Don't go yet! Wait a minute!"

Hopping on his crutch, he immediately gives chase. Napoleon has nearly reached the village when he finally catches up with him, grabbing him by his coattails in a last desperate lunge.

Napoleon turns around and looks at him, stony-faced. The small pale man is now livid with a cold fury that would make anyone else beat a hasty retreat. Not so Edmond the Veteran, who withstands his stare without twitching a muscle, then moves into the attack. "Well? . . ." he drawls, drawing out the syllable with a sort of crapulous familiarity.

"Well what?" Napoleon replies tersely, a little taken aback by his aplomb.

"Well, are you going off like that, without leaving something for the guide?"

Napoleon throws him a five-sou coin. With arrogant nonchalance, the cripple slips it into his belt, turns around on his crutch, and, without so much as a backward glance, makes his exit from the scene.

NAPOLEON FEELS very thirsty. He goes and sits on the terrace of the Café de la Grande Armée.

The girl who had spoken to him that morning comes to serve him.

She has the indefinable feeling that this man is somewhat different from the customers she usually sees here. When ordering his beer, he scarcely looks at her. His whole demeanor possesses a sort of haughty courtesy that both intimidates and delights her.

He is eating a bread roll that he has taken out of his pocket, like a pauper. And yet—she is sure of it—this man has nothing in common with the penny-pinching tourists who bring their own food to save the price of a meal.

Ordinarily she can't stand such people, but this time it's different, quite different—but she can't really say why. He absentmindedly breaks his bread with his plump white hands. His gestures have the unctuous solemnity of a clergyman.

She brings him a plate and a knife, so that he can eat his bread properly. She hovers around his table, wanting to start up a conversation.

"Have you seen the bedroom . . . ?" she begins, but suddenly remembers that she already made this suggestion when he first passed by, and she fears that he may misunderstand her and suspect that she wants to make him spend more or that she is indirectly trying to make him ashamed of ordering so little. She blushes violently at the very thought that he could misjudge her in that way and corrects herself at once. "Have you seen the battlefield?"

"I've just come from there."

"Oh, if I'd only known, I could have been your guide!"

"Thank you. To tell the truth, I did come across a sort of guide, an army veteran who . . ."

"Oh no! You don't mean Edmond? . . . But Edmond's a charlatan! And did he make you pay? How much did the old crook get out of you? I hate to tell you this, but he's always trying to impress the tourists with tales of his missing leg. His famous leg! He tells people that it was shot off by a cannonball, and he even shows them a rusty old piece of shot—purple with his blood, so he says—which he keeps in his hut. He probably showed it to you, eh? You mustn't believe him. Everything he says is a pack of lies, but he can't fool us. The truth is that one night, when he was dead drunk, he tumbled into a ditch and gashed his leg so badly that in the end the maggots got into it and he had to go to the bone setter in Maransart, who cut it off. And ever since, he tells the visitors that he lost it in the battle. Edmond the Veteran of Waterloo! Ha! ha!" (she bursts out laughing like a schoolgirl, with her hand over her mouth). "He's an awful liar, you know!"

"I gathered as much," Napoleon replies, quite composed. Changing the subject, he inquires about ways of getting to France. She informs him that the mail coach to Charleroi is due at about four o'clock. He can quite comfortably spend the night in Charleroi and from there take the old bone shaker to the border.

After finishing his second bread roll, he stretches out his legs and closes his eyes. He still has plenty of time to take a nap in the shade.

He muses. He has always had the unshakable conviction that all the setbacks that have happened in his life, even those that seemed the most painful and futile, must in some way or another actively contribute to the working out of his destiny. There is no doubt in his mind that the bizarre pilgrimage he made that morning was also part of that mysterious grand design, but for the moment he gives up any attempt at exploring its obscure significance. Perhaps it was necessary to stir up the shadows of a vanished past in order to realize more clearly that, from now on, the only true Napoleon is the one who belongs to the future—a future that awaits him in Paris!

III · AN INCIDENT
AT THE BORDER

THE OLD COACH has been traveling for many
hours. It was already on its way by the early
morning, when the birds began to call; it has
rumbled through the calm of noon, allowing
the passengers only twenty minutes' rest in an
empty inn, silent and full of flies. It has traveled
throughout the afternoon, until the sudden chill
at dusk reminds the travelers that the warmth
of the day has merely been the caprice of an
early spring.

The hustle and bustle of the journey surges
around Napoleon, who sits rock-like, calm and
concentrated. His traveling companions have
been busy lighting cigars, striking up conver-
sations, unfolding newspapers, uncorking bot-

tles, peeling hard-boiled eggs, slicing sausages, taking off overcoats, untying scarves, unbuttoning waistcoats, shedding flannel underwear, exchanging confidences, telling bawdy jokes, criticizing the government, and providing physiological details about their state of health. Eventually the cool of the evening has made them progressively button up again. Some are already nodding, their noses buried in their overcoats, while dusk, creeping over the fields, deepens into night.

Impervious to heat and cold, to the pleasures of tobacco and conversation, Napoleon has stuck stoically to his diet of dry bread and daydreams. His imagination is galloping far ahead of the four horses whose hooves monotonously pound the highway for hours on end—toward Paris, toward Paris!

"FLEURUS! Royal Gendarmerie patrol! Passport check!"

Under the light of the coach lamp, in a halo of mist, a gendarme's busby covered in tiny droplets of rain appears framed in the window. Only his face, red with cold, and the golden glow of the button on his collar stand out in the blackness of the night that has covered the whole countryside like the lid on a cauldron.

The travelers stretch, shake themselves, and shiver, hunching their shoulders under this sudden intrusion of cold and silence. They feel as though they are lost on another planet. The only sounds to be heard are the peaceful breathing of the team of horses, the clinking of a bit, the scraping of a horseshoe.

The gendarme buries his nose in the crumpled papers that have been handed to him. A stubborn smoker lights up his old cigar again, filling the coach with its acrid stench.

"Lenormand, Eugène Lenormand. Which one of you is he?" the gendarme asks, waving a passport in his hand.

The passengers start looking at each other suspiciously.

"Well, where's Lenormand?" the gendarme repeats, growing impatient.

The inconspicuous passenger in the gray coat suddenly gives a start, like someone who has just woken up. This slight shiver is a sufficient clue for the anxious and surly bourgeois who are traveling with him; in fact, they have

49

identified him even before he can do so himself. "Come on, can't you hear Monsieur le Gendarme calling you? What are you waiting for?" All these peremptory looks in his direction: they must be right.

"Get down," says the gendarme. "Follow me."

His legs are stiff and he has difficulty making his way to the door between two rows of hostile whispering passengers. The gendarme helps him down.

The old coach has started off again. The yellow lamp that dangles on its rear jumps each time it goes over a bump in the road. Then the light disappears, suddenly snuffed out by a bend in the road.

Napoleon allows himself to be led like a blind man to the guardhouse, a cottage by the side of the road, half hidden behind a fence. A dog barks in the dark. His chain can be heard grating against a wooden post.

Inside the guardhouse, two gendarmes are smoking their pipes in front of a cast-iron stove. A sergeant in his shirtsleeves is sitting behind a kitchen table. He looks rather like a balding bailiff. His boots are lying in a corner and he is wearing slippers. The usual pot of geraniums sits on the windowsill. Apart from the smell of tobacco and old socks, the atmosphere in the room, all things considered, is more like a cozy bourgeois interior than a police station.

"Sergeant, we've got the man!" the gendarme announces, looking pleased with himself.

The Man! This is what all the crowned heads of Europe used to call him, in fear and trembling, as though the four syllables of his Christian name were a thunderbolt that could topple their thrones at the first distant rumble . . .

"Eugène Lenormand, wanted for failure to pay a bill. You left the hotel Au Rendezvous des Namurois, at the wooden clock in the rue du Théâtre in Brussels . . ." The sergeant was reading from a document in front of him, as though giving evidence. He placed his finger on the last word and looked up at the accused. Meanwhile, the gendarme who had detained him went over to the stove and, with a look of utter contentment, stood with the tails of his jacket lifted, warming his back.

The offense was trivial and the offender unimportant. The other gendarmes yawned. Only the sergeant went on looking at Napoleon closely and thoughtfully. The two men stared at each other in silence for quite some time.

"You'll be taken back to Charleroi tomorrow morning," the sergeant said at last in his toneless voice. He slipped into the table drawer the offender's papers, which the gendarme had handed over when he came in. "For tonight, you can put him with Louis," the sergeant added, turning to the gendarme.

Napoleon had not uttered a single word. The gendarme indicated that he wanted him to follow, and they found themselves once more out in the cold night air. As they walked around the cottage, they passed behind the fence. A big dog bounded out of its kennel, pulling on its chain. It was about to give another series of barks, but at the gendarme's command growled and curled up in its shelter.

They crossed the vegetable garden and arrived at a sort of outhouse—probably an old toolshed. The gendarme unbolted the door and guided Napoleon inside. In the dark, he pointed out his bed: a bed made of wooden planks on which Napoleon could feel the rough thickness of a folded blanket.

The gendarme went out, and Napoleon heard him put a padlock on the outside.

Napoleon sat down on the bed while his eyes got accustomed to the dark, but he could make out only the vague, pale shape of a tiny skylight above his head.

It was relatively warm in the confined space of the hut, and a faint smell of cattle hung in the air.

He was getting ready to explore the place by groping around in the dark, when he suddenly became aware of an unknown presence in the room. A few yards away, in the opposite corner, there was a noise like a heavy body turning over in its sleep on a bed of straw. The other occupant of the shed kept on tossing about on his straw, exhaling very loudly two or three times like a surfacing whale, then seemed to sink back into the depths of silent sleep.

It must be Louis, Napoleon thought, remembering what the sergeant had said. But who on earth was Louis? A warder or another prisoner? A tramp, a drunk? Or perhaps it wasn't a man at all but some large animal, an ox, who knows? In this state of uncertainty, he decided to keep quiet, and without making a sound he lay down on the wooden bed. He did not take off his clothes but merely loosened his cravat. He covered himself with the rough blanket and, lying flat on his back, waited for sleep to come.

Sleep did not come. His body was nearly collapsing with fatigue, but his mind, as effervescent as ever, was still burning brightly like a forgotten chandelier in a ruined house.

With his eyes wide open he tried to penetrate the darkness of the hut. Turning his head slightly, he noticed that the dull white of the square window was now more pronounced. Perhaps the moon had risen, or was it frost?

His mind worked feverishly. The hotel bill —what was the stupid place called again? Something to do with Luxembourgeois?—he would pay the hotel bill, and the fine, and anything else he had to. He did not have much money left, but that was not the real problem. What terrified him was the fact that they would want to check his identity, and his rather crudely forged papers would never stand up to any kind of close inspection. What a fate! He had straddled oceans and scaled mountains, only to slip in a puddle of water or stumble over a molehill.

At that moment, Louis seemed to stir again on his straw.

. . . What a fate! To sink within sight of the harbor; to end his epic struggle here in this . . . this Belgian rabbit hutch, beside a . . . beside this . . . but who the devil was this Louis? His mysterious neighbor had gone to sleep again without emitting any sounds that could identify him. No matter, he would see who this creature was in the morning—and besides, why should this ridiculous companion be of any concern to him? . . . Sleep claimed him at last.

WHEN HE OPENED his eyes again, the gray light that comes before dawn was filling the shed. Sitting up, he was astonished to see that the door was open. The room was much smaller than he had imagined. A heap of gardening tools draped in cobwebs and a big garden umbrella dotted with pigeon droppings occupied one corner. In the other was a straw litter with a faded red horse blanket lying across it. The ceiling was made of badly joined boards that formed a loft, where cooing pigeons could be heard pattering about on their tiny, soft feet.

Napoleon got up cautiously. His limbs were numb. The cold air made him shiver. He was unsure whether to go out. Wasn't this open door some sort of a trap?

Just as he had finally decided to try his luck, a person who obviously had been waiting for this signal to make his entrance suddenly burst into the hut.

It was the sergeant. His face was transfigured. He seemed to be overcome by such intense excitement that it was hard to recognize the nondescript official of the previous evening.

He rushed toward Napoleon, dropped down on one knee, and seizing his hand he kissed it, saying in a voice choked with emotion: "Sire! Sire! You've come back at last!"

After quickly hiding his initial surprise, the Emperor, now very much in control of himself, graciously placed a hand on the gendarme's shoulder and raised him to his feet again.

For a long while the two men stood facing each other in silence. The pigeons could still be heard quietly walking about above their heads.

Breathtaking encounter! Unforgettable moment! Indescribable emotion!

How many times had Napoleon imagined situations like this in his dreams of returning to France! In actual fact, the only real surprise was to discover how similar this scene was to everything he had already imagined, so similar that he almost had the feeling of living through it for the second time.

In a hurried whisper, the sergeant apologized profusely: last night he had had to lodge his Emperor in a most unworthy fashion, but it had been the only way to ensure his safety and protect him from any indiscreet curiosity on the part of the other gendarmes. He had sent them to patrol the Fleurus highway before dawn, so the two of them were alone for the moment. However, there was not a minute to lose.

He led Napoleon back into the empty guard-house, got him to gulp down a big bowl of coffee, and slipped some bread, two hard-boiled eggs, and a piece of cheese into the pocket of his overcoat for the journey. "I'm going to take some shortcuts to get you across the border. I'll leave you on the road to Valenciennes, and when I come back I'll explain to my men that I took you to Charleroi police station myself. As for your file which came from Brussels, there'll be no further action on that—I just have to dispose of the report of your arrest. Here are your papers. Now, let's make a start as soon as possible."

For safety's sake, the sergeant asked Napoleon to walk in front of his horse while they were on the highway, in the fashion a gendarme usually leads a prisoner.

Then they took a track across country with Napoleon up behind the sergeant on the same horse. They covered a good two leagues at a brisk pace, following low-lying roads, taking shortcuts across pastures where the cows took little notice of them, passing plowed fields, and avoiding the few villages by constantly keeping under the cover of the thick woods which dotted the countryside.

The sergeant pulled his horse to a halt at the top of a hill crowned with poplars. From the place where they stood, a cart track consisting of two ruts overgrown with grass wound its lazy way around the curve of the hill and descended toward the plain. In the haze of early dawn, a vast plain spread out in front of them; far away in the distance, one could vaguely see the blue shape of one or two large towns with their steeples and belfries.

The sergeant jumped down from his horse and helped Napoleon dismount. The horse was exhausted and steaming. It snorted loudly, then began to graze along the slope.

Dawn was turning into day.

"Sire, you are now in France!"

Napoleon let his eyes wander for a moment over this soft gray expanse. There was not the slightest breath of wind. He felt warmer now after the ride. Then he turned toward his guide, who was respectfully standing two paces behind him.

There were a thousand things the sergeant wanted to say, but his throat went dry. Never, even in his wildest dreams, had he ever imagined that one day he could have a private conversation like this with his Emperor, but now he felt those indescribable moments whirling away from him before he had had the chance to express the emotion that filled his heart.

And what of Napoleon? To tell the truth, at that moment his mind was occupied, much against his will, with a thought so futile that he himself was irritated by it: *Who on earth was Louis?* Resisting this stupid obsession, inappropriate to the solemnity of the occasion, he finally asked, "What is your name, my good man?"

"Bommel. Bommel, Justin. Ex-company sergeant-major in the 1st Infantry Regiment of the Départements du Nord. I was at Waterloo . . . well, almost . . ." he added, stumbling over the last words. If he had not been at Waterloo, it was certainly through no fault of his own. The recruits from the north had been mobilized at the last moment and arrived too late to take part in the action. Napoleon knows all that, and many other things besides. He can read this simple fellow's face like an open book: it tells of a lifetime of frustrated hopes and dogged loyalty. This man is truly one of the faithful. Napoleon commits his name to memory; one day, he will be able to show his appreciation.

Bommel has an inspiration that suddenly loosens his tongue. "In Paris you could get in touch with my friend Second Lieutenant Truchaut, who lives in the Impasse-des-Chevaliers-du-Temple. He's absolutely loyal to the cause. He ekes out a meager living on his half-pension; in the eyes of the local bourgeois, he's just a poor devil, not worthy of any particular attention. For this very reason, you would be quite safe with him. He will certainly be able to offer you accommodation. And besides, he knows all the veterans of the Imperial Army in Paris . . ."

He stops short, suddenly frightened by his own audacity. Since when did the Eagle need the help of sparrows to build his eyrie? Wasn't it impudent and ridiculous to imagine for one moment that Napoleon would need to rely on the likes of Bommels and Truchauts? Overcome by the sense of his own unworthiness, the poor man has already forgotten that if the Emperor had managed to escape complete disaster in Belgium, it was entirely due to him! Napoleon, however, has made a more accurate assessment of the situation and, far from being offended by the gendarme's naïve concern, has carefully taken note of Second Lieutenant Truchaut's name and address.

There was no time to waste; they now had to go their separate ways.

Sparrows were chirping noisily among the brambles in the ditches. The sky was pale green in the east. A crescent moon still hung low in the sky, forgotten, just above the black fields.

The sergeant attempted to give a military salute, but Napoleon, with a magnanimous gesture, opened his arms and embraced him.

The sergeant mounted his horse. Napoleon watched the rider's silhouette until it disappeared completely over the other side of the hill, then looked once more at the far horizon, where the dawn mists were beginning to lift.

So, he was back in France!

It is a strange thing but, whether from fatigue or because there was no one to witness it, he could not summon up the surge of emotion he should have felt on such a historic occasion. Nevertheless, this emotional sterility only made

him all the more fiercely and implacably determined.

He pissed pensively against a fence post,
carefully straightened his clothes, which had
been crumpled by the early-morning ride, and
strode down toward the plain.

IV · WATERMELONS

& CANTALOUPES

FROM PROVENCE

IN PARIS, spring was already well on the way. All over the city, the buds on the plane trees and chestnut trees were bursting out into soft green tufts.

On such a glorious day, the Impasse-des-Chevaliers-du-Temple looked almost like a country lane. Only the first half of it was paved; the end was lost among the grass and brambles of a vacant lot that looked like a big garden run wild.

On the edge of this meadow, already humming with bees, the last house in the street stood alone. A sign was painted in large letters on its front wall:

An empty cart rested, shafts up, against the wall near the door.

Not many people could have come there, for the arrival of a stranger on that late afternoon created considerable excitement among a few hens dozing on the old cart.

As he got nearer to the house, the visitor, who was somewhat shortsighted, finally noticed with a start that above the sign painted on the wall were a few words in smaller letters:

Widow Truchaut & Partners

He stood still and, head down, appeared to be deep in thought. Or was he just catching his breath? Although he had no luggage, his crumpled coat and dusty boots seemed to indicate that he had undergone a long, tiring journey.

He looked intently all about him; then, after a moment's hesitation, went up the four steps that led to the door of the house.

The door was ajar. Through the gap wafted

the smell of ripe fruit—as mellow as a memory of summers past.

The visitor banged loudly on the door twice with his closed fist. After a moment's silence he heard the shuffle of slippers on the flagstones. Then the door opened wide, revealing a woman with a bright, happy face. She was about forty, tall and rather ungainly, though not ugly—more exactly, she still had a certain youth and vigor which, combined with an air of kindness, took the place of beauty.

She looked at the stranger, slightly puzzled.

"I . . . I've just come back from a long trip and I was hoping to find Second Lieutenant Truchaut here, but I've only just noticed outside the, er, the sign that . . ."

"Ah yes, sir. My poor Truchaut! He passed away nearly two years ago, the dear man!" The widow spoke with a broad Provençal accent. "Were you a friend of his? Are you an army man, too?"

"I didn't know him personally, but we had friends in common, old comrades from the Grande Armée. But I haven't introduced myself: Lieutenant Lenormand, artillery."

"Come in, do come in. We mustn't stand on

the doorstep like this. Have you been traveling long? Ah, my dear Truchaut, the poor dear man, how happy he would have been to see you! Nowadays, you know, there are not many left who've remained faithful to the Emperor and proud to have served him! Actually, they'd rather hide the fact in their eagerness to chase a cushy job here, a pension there . . . But Truchaut, now he was true to the end, a wonderful man! He always wore his cross—they buried it with him. 'I'd rather starve,' he always used to say, 'than desert the Emperor.' He really believed that the Emperor would return. There were a few of them, real fanatics who never gave up, but what good people! Talking of starving—I can tell you, that's just what happened to him, or near enough. Selling pumpkins won't keep a man, specially in times like these which are so difficult for people who refuse to knuckle under. Besides, to be frank, he wasn't cut out for business. And of course, he had to devote himself to his real mission in life, as he used to call it. Politics took up all his time and energy. It was the same for his friends. You'll meet them, I'll introduce you. There's the medical officer, Dr. Lambert-Laruelle, Sergeant Maurice, and the others. They're always at the café, Les Trois Boules. To look at them, you'd think they were men of leisure playing their usual game of cards. Between you and me, I think they were plotting something. But I'm a woman and a soldier's wife. I know better than to poke my nose where it's not wanted. Truchaut wasn't one to talk, and I certainly wouldn't have tried to worm information out of him. When he came home from Les Trois Boules looking worried, I wouldn't have dared speak to him about the business and bother him with my petty worries about monthly bills, settlement dates, and so on. Although, heaven knows there were times when it would have been such a relief to confide in him and tell him all my business problems. You see, I'm the one who looks after the business. It's just a small concern that I began from nothing: my cousins are farmers in Avignon. They send their fruit to Paris and we try to sell it where we can. In theory, it should work, but what can I do, there's no one but me to run the whole thing; I had no experience, and I can't really cope on my own. And that's not taking into account the kids and everything else that has to be done.

Truchaut wasn't cut out to be a greengrocer: he was a gifted man, a man of ideas, a thinker, a politician if you like. And what a speaker! You should have heard him sometimes in the evening. Sometimes when I'd finished my work, I'd go and seek him out at Les Trois Boules. Oh, you should've heard him, you should've seen him! It was wonderful! 'Be careful, Truchaut,' they used to say, 'not so loud, that's enough, you never know who's listening!' They told him to shut up, but at the same time they wanted to keep on listening to him, and anyway, he was not easily intimidated. Shut up indeed! Bold as you like, he would shout all the louder, and we sat there listening to him—we would have listened to him all night. Of course, after all that, when we were back home, how could I start talking shop! I wouldn't have dared, I couldn't have done it, and that's that! However much I said to myself, This time there's no getting out of it, I must talk to him about Bongrain's bill and the shipment that went bad in transit . . . I just couldn't, because I knew he was a man with a mission. Sadly, he's dead now, and his friends aren't young anymore. Besides, they never had the same vitality as my dear Truchaut, and now that he's gone, they've really lost heart, my business is practically ruined, and the Emperor is still on his godforsaken island. Ah, dear me! But life goes on just the same . . . Get off there!" With one sweep of her arm, she brushed a brown hen off the table, where it had been picking at a stray vegetable peeling. "But here I am talking my head off and I haven't even asked you to sit down. What am I thinking of? Make yourself at home. You must be thirsty. There's nothing left in the house, but even when there's nothing in the house, there's still a cool jug of rosé in the cellar. I'll fetch it for you."

She went down to the cellar.

Napoleon sank down onto a stool and looked about him. The room was cool and spacious, with a high ceiling, which made it seem very bare. The floor was paved with cracked, uneven blue flagstones, and the only furniture in the room was a long wooden table, a few stools, and a cupboard. In one corner some iron trunks were piled up beside two or three crates and a big cane basket. In the darkest corner, two dozen cantaloupes lined up on the floor smelled of sun and summer. Various pieces of phantom furniture were outlined in white against the gray of the bare walls: rectangles of different sizes suggested vanished wardrobes, invisible dressers, and there was even the oval shape of what must have been a large mirror. All that had no doubt been seized by the bailiffs and then disappeared under the auctioneer's hammer.

Widow Truchaut took up again where she had left off, even before she had emerged from the cellar stairs. She must have been starved of conversation for quite a while. "Then, finally, I had to tell him about the situation we were in, but it was too late. He was already very ill—his liver, his stomach, nothing was functioning properly, not to mention the shrapnel wound in his back that still troubled him. But Truchaut was a fighter by nature; his body had given up long ago, but he had great self-control; it was always mind over matter. What spirit! At heart he was a great idealist, as the medical officer, Dr. Lambert-Laruelle, used to say. He was like a man possessed. But he burned the candle at both ends. And then, when his health finally broke down—*fftt*—it was all over in a few days. One morning he lay down there on the old sofa"—she pointed toward a whitish horizontal outline on the empty wall—"and never got up again. He was still conscious, but didn't speak again. Or was he really conscious? I couldn't be certain. His eyes were wide open but lifeless, as if he wasn't really seeing anything. It was probably just as well, really. He didn't even seem to notice when the men came to take all our stuff away. Those ruffians would have snatched the sofa from under him if, in the end, I hadn't kicked them out so that he could at least die in peace before they looted everything! . . . Ah yes, sir, that's how he left us, and since then nothing has gone right, but don't let that stop you from having a drink."

She took a mug out of the cupboard. As the door opened and shut, Napoleon could see that it was pitifully empty. She filled the mug to the brim with rosé.

The wine was cool and lively on the tongue. Her voice, even when she was describing disasters, still had a kind of cheerfulness. In the midst of ruination, this woman radiated a warmth and vitality which could be felt in the old house itself, in spite of its being so bare.

She talked at great length, pouring out her heart. He found himself listening without any impatience as she described the exploits of the late Second Lieutenant Truchaut, his companions, and their barroom conspiracies. Not that he was at all interested in what she said, but he drew an odd feeling of comfort from her cheerful energy, while the rosé, consumed on an empty stomach after a tiring journey, filled him with unusual benevolence. Sitting close to this simple soul, in the big room with its stone floor polished with age, watching it slowly filling with the soft shadows of evening, he had the feeling that, after drifting for so many months, he was for the first time on solid ground again.

IT WAS NOT UNTIL the room was almost dark that a silence fell at last. The visitor had no desire to take his leave. He could not face the prospect of departing from this unexpected haven and continuing his endless wandering in the cold indifference of unfamiliar streets. But how could he induce Widow Truchaut to offer him a bed for the night?

As he was vainly mulling this question over in his mind, a surprising turn of events suddenly came to his rescue.

All at once the sound of children's voices was heard in the street. The door was flung open and half a dozen scruffy kids rushed into the room in a state of high excitement.

"You rascals!" screamed Widow Truchaut, full of motherly indignation, her hand raised ready to give them a clout. "Can't you see I have a visitor? You monkeys!"

"Ostrich, Ostrich! Listen, listen!" the children squealed in their shrill voices, but as they were all shouting at once, it was impossible to understand anything.

Then three men, breathing hard, burst into the room. The last of the three shut the door carefully behind him. Silence. The children, who had been their advance guard, were now huddled together against the wall, all aquiver with the special thrill that children feel at the news that some major catastrophe has occurred in the world of adults.

Napoleon's eyes were now accustomed to the darkness of the room, and he easily guessed who the newcomers were—their bearing alone betrayed their background. The tall beardless one with the horseman's rolling gait was probably Sergeant Maurice, whom the widow had mentioned earlier; the bald head and the potbelly no doubt belonged to the medical officer, Dr. Latruelle-Something. As to the last of the trio, he had the swollen features of an absinthe drinker. His face, as worn as an old doormat, had the vacuous look so typical of loyal old soldiers who have never risen above the ranks.

"Ostrich . . ." The medical officer began to speak in a hoarse, solemn voice. (A moment ago Napoleon had been shocked to hear the children addressing the widow in this manner. Now, however, from the serious way the newcomer used the nickname, he presumed that the bad joke was of such ancient origin that it had lost any humorous connotation.) The medical officer stopped: he had just noticed the presence of a stranger in the room.

"You can speak freely, Major," the Ostrich said, "he's one of us." She introduced Lieutenant Lenormand. The three men shook hands with him silently and very solemnly, as one does at a funeral.

"Ostrich . . ." the medical officer continued,

his voice more husky than ever, "and you, comrade," he added, turning to Napoleon, "the news that I must . . . that we have just . . . Oh, read it for yourselves . . ." He took from his pocket a sheet of newspaper almost rolled into a ball, which no one could have deciphered in the growing darkness, and collapsed onto a stool, his head bowed, his fingers working the crumpled paper into a rag.

Then, in doleful chorus, the beardless horseman and the nameless drunkard finished for him: "Ladies and gentlemen, alas! The Emperor is dead."

V · THE CONQUEST

OF PARIS

THE NEWS, which had struck Napoleon like a thunderbolt, shocked him even more deeply than his companions—though there were naturally very different reasons for his dismay.

He had no trouble playing the part during the funeral vigil which took place that evening at the Ostrich's house. The personal fate of his double scarcely affected him (to tell the truth, he felt intense annoyance at this idiot who, entrusted with a unique mission, had carelessly allowed himself to die at a time when he was still needed); but he had only to consider the consequences of that disastrous death to be able with no pretense whatsoever to give an impression of utter consternation to the assembled company. At the same time, he was touched to see the sincere emotion of those who surrounded him. The thought that these humble people could be so overcome by the mere idea that he was dead moved him so much that his tears flowed effortlessly with theirs.

It was a long vigil. They wept, talked, drank. That night, a strange intimacy, forged from their common grief, bound together these old children who found themselves all at once orphans of the same dream. In their helplessness, they clung ever closer together, and when it was finally time to get some rest, they could not reconcile themselves to the idea of sending this brother in arms, whom fate had so recently entrusted to them, off into the profane indifference of the outside world. So it was quite natural that Napoleon should accept the improvised bed which they made for him out of old rags heaped up in a corner of the big room. The medical officer, who boarded with the widow, insisted on giving him his mattress. The lugubrious cavalryman and the nameless drunkard took their leave; they shared a garret somewhere near the cul-de-sac.

The Ostrich prodded the stumbling flock of

sleepy children toward the stairs. The medical officer retired to his own room. The Ostrich came down again to provide Napoleon with an extra eiderdown.

When the whole house was finally fast asleep, Napoleon blew out his candle and lay down. Somewhere in the neighborhood the first roosters of the dawn were beginning their fanfare. He shivered: from now on *his destiny was posthumous.*

IN THE DAYS THAT FOLLOWED, the full horror of his new situation became clearer still.

In a Europe which could not find a single adversary worthy of opposing him, the dismemberment of states, the carving up of empires, the dethronement of kings were hardly challenges to him . . . But now an obscure noncommissioned officer, simply by dying like a fool on a deserted rock at the other end of the world, had managed to confront him with the most formidable and unexpected rival imaginable: himself! Worse still, from now on Napoleon would have to make his way not only against Napoleon, but against a Napoleon who was larger than life—the memory of Napoleon!

As the medical officer, who had been only too happy to find someone to share the dull emptiness of his days, took him on his rounds of the faithful during the following week, he was in a better position to gauge the full extent of the disaster. Those old soldiers, the stoical officers on half-pay, the rank and file, sustained by an unshakable hope, had spent the last six years waiting for the Emperor's return, and would have risen up in a body at the first call. Now, at one stroke, his passing away had de-mobilized all those humble foot soldiers of the imperial cause, every one of them.

Now that it had been dissipated, how could all that immense energy be harnessed again? The degree of prostration felt by the faithful was all the greater because they had made such superhuman efforts to survive all those years without wavering in their resolution. And to-day, perhaps this sudden extinction of all their reasons to hope and believe even brought them a certain grim sense of relief . . . They enjoyed their despair: they sank into it with a kind of relish, as one voluptuously sinks into sleep after a very long vigil. If anyone had tried to wake them at that time, he would have found them not only deaf but hostile as well. Relieved from the rigors of guard duty, released from the double burden of loyalty and hope, free at last, they drifted among memories. Now that they had succumbed to the poison of nostalgia, they wallowed in the past; who could ever persuade them to become once again those galley slaves of glory, chained together by a common dream that was perhaps an illusion?

And who would ever recognize him, now that there was no longer anyone to wait for him? The transformation brought about by age and the indignity of his disguise, which a few days earlier had not been sufficient to screen him from the eyes of a true believer, would from now on stand as a barrier between himself and his followers. Should he wear himself out in an effort to convince them and win them back again one by one, and then endlessly try to patch up the cracks in their crumbling support—should he eternally devote himself to propping up the irreparably damaged structure of their faith, when all he had was his presence and his words? He felt his strength fail him at the thought of the enormous task that awaited him.

. . . At the same time, he itched to see action again. His situation as the Ostrich's temporary boarder became more delicate day by day. To justify it, he would have to reveal his true identity, and that was something he could not do. It was both too early and too late to play his only card. Any premature attempt to impose upon his simple companions a truth that they were no longer equipped to bear, that they were not yet ready to bear, could condemn him to failure and intolerable derision. He was well aware of that. He worried and fretted in his useless refuge: the more urgent the need to act, the clearer it became that action was impossible.

It was then that a fresh delivery of watermelons and cantaloupes from Avignon suddenly changed the course of his fate.

The sweet-smelling freight—there were two cartloads of it—had been spread out on the tiled floor of the big room. For some days, the Ostrich, helped by the gang of children and a few ex-soldiers from Les Trois Boules, had been in a flurry of activity, trying to retail this merchandise along the streets. The little band went out at dawn and returned late at night, exhausted and demoralized. Sales were poor, the pile of cantaloupes that occupied three-quarters of the room didn't seem to get any smaller. And, like a sinister portent, here and there a cantaloupe was already beginning to go soft.

One afternoon, as Napoleon was gloomily turning over his thoughts while walking up and down the room—or at any rate the narrow space that had remained unencumbered—he accidentally trod on a watermelon, slid, and lurched wildly.

He nearly sprained his ankle. The melon squashed open, spreading its juicy entrails across the tiles and releasing an odor of rotting fruit.

As he stood, staring dumbly at the sticky mess that had spurted out onto this boot, he was suddenly overcome by a surge of fury. The oppressive smell of the melons, the insistent buzzing of the flies, the frantic, well-meaning

efforts of the Ostrich and her inept assistants
—the reality of everything that he had hitherto
registered only passively, suddenly hit him in
the face like an insult; he was no longer the
cold and detached spectator of this mediocre
farce; thrown out of his illusory box seat, he
was horrified to discover that the pitiful hero
of the piece was none other than himself. For
the first time, he began to see himself as he
really was, naked and defenseless at the center
of a universal debacle, buffeted this way and
that by events, threatened on every side by an
all-pervasive decay, sinking slowly into the
quicksands of failed resolutions, and finally disappearing into the ultimate morass against
which no honor could prevail. He suddenly lost
his self-control; in an explosion of rage and
revolt, he grabbed the burst watermelon and
hurled it at the wall. It squashed there and
formed a star which slowly began to dribble
down . . .

. . . Like the sky which is cleansed by a storm,
he found himself wonderfully purged by this
sudden outburst. He was already beginning to
see in a different light the wretched melon that
only a moment before had set his morbid train

of thought in motion: his mind had just hit on a new inspiration.

That evening, when the Ostrich and her troop came back to the house, they were all struck by the sudden change in him. They were in the presence of another man entirely: in the place of yesterday's self-effacing boarder, they found a leader.

He addressed them briefly. His words were clear and simple, with a ring of authority that electrified them. He pointed out that the stock of overripe melons was their only capital, perhaps the last card in their hand; that they could not afford to play it haphazardly, as they had been doing up till now, in an effort that was most certainly brave but confused and futile; that, on the contrary, it was imperative to prepare their plan of action thoughtfully, with painstaking attention to detail, so that they could then concentrate all their energy in one decisive move, carried out at the most opportune time and place.

Instinctively he recovered the language of the army leader speaking to his generals on the eve of battle, and those grave but powerful tones immediately struck a chord in his audience. They spontaneously invited him to take command of operations, and asked him to explain his plan in detail.

He asked for a Paris street map and spread it out on the table. The Ostrich lit some extra candles. The whole troop sat in a circle around the table. Only Napoleon remained standing. After a long, hard look at the map, he walked up and down the room for a few minutes, his hands behind his back. No one dared to break the silence. In the candlelight his short silhouette cast shadows to the four corners of the wall, shadows that seemed to leap from a giant spring. Finally, after sending a stray pumpkin sailing into the air with a short sharp kick, he turned around on the spot, and like an eagle diving on its prey, he came back to the table and in front of his troops outlined the following strategy:

1. The time factor
The heat wave which we are now experiencing does not, on the face of it, favor our campaign, since it makes the melons ripen quickly. In reality, it also contains an element that could benefit us, one we

should exploit to the full, and that is the thirst it creates in the townspeople. If we act swiftly *there is nothing to stop us from turning these weather conditions to our advantage. Indeed, swiftness of action will allow us to make use of the inherent advantages of the situation (i.e., the increased thirst of potential customers), and to avoid the harmful effects (progressive stock loss through spoilage).*

2. The terrain factor

I have no need to remind you that Paris covers a wide area and that we have only minimal forces at our disposal to sweep the field. An uncoordinated, haphazard effort would therefore be certain to fail. First, we must determine all the regions where the lie of the land could work against us: long, quiet streets in districts where our column would risk losing precious time and where the ardor of its initial impetus would be dulled without achieving any gain; les Halles, markets, the vicinity of greengrocers' shops—all areas where the inhabitants show a stronger buyer resistance because there is so much stiff competition—these various points must be totally excluded from our itinerary [as he spoke, he seized a pencil and, with a decisive cross, eliminated les Halles from the map]. *We shall therefore concentrate our strength exclusively in those regions that offer the least pos-*

sibility of resistance and the best chance of gaining a prompt, significant advantage with the greatest economy of effort—i.e., the zones that present both a maximum concentration of population and a minimum supply level of fruit and vegetables. As regards the first aspect (population), from now on, we can concentrate on the central districts and mark the most frequently used access routes [the pencil authoritatively circled a wide area in the middle of the map, from which it drew out four or five main approaches]. *As regards the second question (finding out the location of fruit shops), it will be imperative to send out scouts to effect a preliminary reconnaissance of the terrain. This reconnaissance will be carried out at dawn, and will hardly delay the launching of our offensive; it will subsequently even allow us to gain a considerable amount of time, since it will avoid useless counter-marches by immediately enabling us to take up the most favorable positions.*

3. The human factor

A. The enemy. The extent of their resistance—as I have just pointed out—relies on a chain of redoubts placed at irregular intervals, which we must systematically avoid; concentrating all our forces in a charge on one of the breaks in this line, we can use this gap to head straight for the soft underbelly of the city. *Once in that central position, we can deploy our forces more or less widely, depending on the conditions of the terrain, so that the area under our control may be progressively extended.*

B. Our forces. First, the scouts: for this reconnaissance mission, a few children should be adequate—their lightness and mobility recommend them for this type of operation. As for the rest, we will form a single column with all the handcarts and even the wheelbarrows at our disposal. Headquarters will be installed in a café in the central zone, its exact location will be decided at the appropriate time. Liaison between headquarters and the various carts engaged in action will also be carried out by the band of children.

This plan of action was adopted to the applause of the assembled company, which, in spite of the rigors of the day just past and the prospect of an even more difficult day to come, felt a thrill of new hope pass through it.

That evening, the half-pay soldiers, instead of going back to their respective garrets, bivouacked at the Ostrich's house, so that they could form their column at dawn without wasteful delays.

Napoleon's words had awakened in them a

mixture of excitement and confidence. They had the vague impression of being on the eve of an unknown adventure; at the same time, with glad surprise, they fell back again into old habits of obedience and readiness. For this night before combat, some bedded down under the table, some on benches, all wearing their boots and rolled in their overcoats, and soon the large room was filled with the sound of their snoring.

Napoleon was deep in thought, his chin in his hand. His eyes sometimes turned back to the map of Paris, still spread out in front of him.

But he was not the only person awake: seated in the dark corner of the hearth, silent, spellbound, drawing on a dead cigar, the medical officer was watching him.

IN SPITE OF all his perspicacity, the turn of events caught the medical officer unawares. Certainly the triumphal day of the melons had confirmed his suspicions: that brilliant, flawless plan of action was completely in line with a strategy which he had known for a long time to be stunningly effective. Once again, its outstanding success came as no surprise. The subsequent recovery of the Ostrich's business was also predictable, even though it was brought about with staggering vigor and speed. But what really astounded and dismayed the medical officer was the upheaval which he now saw taking place in his own life.

The Other Man had taken charge of everything, with an energy and competence one had to admire. After all, it was normal that he should wish personally to supervise accounts, transport, correspondence, personnel, branch offices, advertising, marketing, stock-taking, legal matters, and public relations, since it was he who had succeeded in reviving, transforming, and developing the business; and besides, the medical officer, who was keen on his leisure time, would not for one moment have thought of disputing the Other's right to rack his brains over those endless, boring tasks. Therefore, it was natural enough, in a sense, that the Other had become the undisputed master of the household.

The fact that the Ostrich now sat at the conquering hero's feet was harder to accept for the medical officer; and yet, with considerable effort, he might even have been able to come to terms with this situation: he knew the affectionate nature and spontaneity of that simple, warmhearted woman, and besides, having none too high an opinion of himself, he had never dared to entertain too much hope for his own chances.

His indignation and distress came from a stranger source: what seemed excusable in the Ostrich became a shocking and unforgivable betrayal in the Other. Seeing him accept the widow's favors and calmly settle into his new-found bourgeois prosperity, the medical officer felt as though he had just witnessed the collapse of everything that justified his own existence. He found himself in a position similar to that of a believer to whom God has just revealed the fact that He intends to retire.

And so, at first, in spite of all the signs, he had refused to believe such an outrage. But, living under the same roof, he could not persist indefinitely in ignoring the weight of evidence to the contrary.

To his great dismay, he found himself free all of a sudden. One morning, taking advantage of the Other's absence, he announced to the Ostrich that he had decided to leave. The lack of concern, the seeming indifference with which she greeted the news, precipitated his determination; his decision, which until that moment was still uncertain, now became irrevocable. Seeing that the widow was not even going to ask him to delay his departure, he thereupon made up a story about an inheritance that urgently required his presence in the country.

The ever-obliging Ostrich immediately provided him with some string and two cardboard boxes in which to pack his belongings. While he tied a knot around his things—in spite of the anger which made his fingers tremble, it barely took a few minutes—to his own astonishment, he became aware for the first time of the part that hatred had played in the ties that for more than twenty years had bound him body and soul in the service of that Other Man, and this hatred was in fact so deep that, in suddenly choosing to flee its object for good, he had the wrenching feeling of cutting off an essential part of himself.

The Ostrich wanted to get a servant to take him to the coach, but his baggage was light and he declined the offer. Overcome with a resentment that he could no longer keep in check, he even refused the farewell drink that the good woman offered him. Suddenly he could not bear to prolong his stay under that roof for another minute. The Ostrich could not understand this agitation and naïvely showed her surprise, which made the whole scene all the more painful.

His sudden flight did not take the medical officer very far. When he got to the end of the street, he realized that he had nowhere to go: quite naturally he would end up at Les Trois Boules. So Napoleon had no difficulty in laying hands on him again, and it was in this establishment, toward the end of the afternoon, that he came as a matter of course to find the deserter.

Sitting down at the table in front of him, Napoleon did not bother, even as a formality, to question him about the reasons for his abrupt departure or his supposed inheritance. Calmly, and with that superb ability to brush aside unimportant details—an ability which usually characterizes genius and which is akin in its effects to natural catastrophes—he came straight to the point that concerned him. The medical officer, who, in the meantime, had recovered a degree of composure, tried to stand up to the first assault without flinching.

"You know who I am," said Napoleon. And without leaving him the time to deal with his first statement—for the medical officer would have taken advantage of it to reply, "You are a prosperous melon merchant"—he went on, "And I need you."

The medical officer, avoiding his master's eyes, lit a cigar. "It's too late," he mumbled into his mustache, staring at the bottom of his glass.

"This is the situation," continued Napoleon, pretending not to have heard the last remark —or perhaps it had really escaped his attention, as the pursuit of a brilliant idea usually made him deaf to any comment that did not accord with his own views.

"It's too late," repeated the medical officer in a louder voice. He summoned all his energy, but still did not dare to raise his eyes to the person he was speaking to. While the latter, disconcerted by this obstinate reaction, tapped the table rather impatiently with his plump white hand, the medical officer, like an old cart horse balking for the first time at the touch of the shafts and kicking out blindly in all directions, went on almost in a shout, "It's too late! I tell you, it's too late!"

His voice grew hoarse. His glass was empty; he gulped down the one opposite. He was struggling now, like a desperate man, to preserve this grim new freedom that he had only just won. Hesitantly, he stretched out his arm and gripped Napoleon by the lapel of his frock coat; at last his yellow eyes came to rest, unsteadily meeting the Other's gaze. "Believe me, just concentrate on making your fortune in watermelons and your future will be a thousand times more enviable than you can imagine. You don't believe me? Come on, then, come with me, and YOU'LL SEE! . . ." Then he added more quietly, "It's not far from here," in a voice soft and sly.

He got up. His legs shook, but his grip stayed firm on Napoleon's coat. The latter, rather taken aback, was aware that in the medical officer's present state it was no use starting a discussion. To avoid a scene, he therefore decided to humor this annoying caprice for the moment. There would always be time to speak of serious matters again later, as soon as the absinthe fumes had cleared away.

Without uttering one more word, the medical officer dragged his bemused victim through a series of quiet streets. They crossed a middle-class suburb with detached houses, iron gates, and gardens. Day was ending; the approaching night was lengthening the shadows; soon they would all blend into a single mysterious softness, which would once more endow this petty world with a dreamy depth, redeeming it from banality at last. Somewhere from behind closed shutters came the sound of someone practicing the piano.

Napoleon was becoming more and more impatient, when his guide indicated to him that they had finally arrived. They stood in front of the entrance to a sort of private park whose walls were overhung with the branches of chestnut and linden. The bars of the iron-grille gate were backed by a metal sheet that frustrated prying eyes.

The medical officer must have been a regular visitor, for in spite of the growing darkness, he managed to find without any difficulty a small chain that was hidden under the ivy. A sharp tug produced a grating metallic sound behind the wall, which in turn was followed by the distant tinkling of a bell.

The two men waited for a moment.

"Will you explain to me now . . ." began Napoleon, who could hardly contain his exasperation—but at that precise instant a small door on well-oiled hinges opened silently in the middle of the iron gate.

Following his guide, Napoleon had to step into this kind of rat trap, whether he wanted to or not, and found himself in the deep shadows of a large unkempt garden with a dense grove of trees.

He could scarcely make out the form of the concierge, who closed the gate again behind them, but it seemed to him that this person was wearing a sort of long, grayish dustcoat and a type of round skull cap that gave him a vaguely ecclesiastical air.

They went into the trees, following a winding sandy path which muffled their footsteps. Under the trees, the dusk had already fallen.

At a bend in the path, the medical officer, whose squat silhouette was now discernible only by the red glow on the end of his cigar, turned to Napoleon and whispered in his ear, "I'll go on ahead, wait for me here a moment." And throwing away his cigar, he vanished into the shadows before Napoleon could stop him.

Napoleon was now alone, standing in the middle of the path. All about him, the dense black treetops hid everything from view. High in the branches, flocks of starlings were finally settling down for the night with shrill cries and beating wings.

How long did he wait like that? The medical officer was still not back. The whole thing began to look like a joke in very questionable taste. Napoleon took out his watch, but could not make out the position of the hands against the dim whiteness of the dial. The starlings had ceased their racket. Only the slight murmur of the wind rose intermittently from the dark emptiness of the park, stirring the invisible depths of the foliage.

Napoleon was not a man to allow himself to be led up the garden path for very long. However, he did not want to give up before finding out what the medical officer's intentions were, and so he decided to carry out a general investigation of the area. Following the pale ribbon of the path through the dark wood, he went on deeper into the park.

After he had gone a short way, he could see a hazy light between the tree trunks. Soon he arrived at a wide clearing where a last pallor of day still lingered. In front of him stretched an overgrown lawn in the shape of an amphitheater on top of which he could see the vague outline of a building, its dark mass dotted with only two or three lights. Taking a shortcut across the lawn, where the dew-laden grass soon soaked his shoes and the bottoms of his trousers, he made his way toward the building.

When he was up close, he saw that it was a pretentious construction, a sort of small château, built very high, with ornate moldings that resembled cake decorations, and with a long, low, ramshackle annex on one side, like a shed. The general effect was one of dilapidation.

The lights were on in the shed, and from one of the open windows came the clink of cutlery, suggesting the presence of a large number of people at dinner. A stale odor of cooking floated in the air; it smelled like a camp kitchen.

Napoleon hesitated to go farther. He stood in the shade of an elm on the edge of the lawn near a bench. He sat down, shivering on contact with the stone, which was wet with dew.

The noise of the cutlery ceased. There was a sound of footsteps and chairs being moved. The door of the shed opened and in the rectangle of light a silhouette appeared, draped in a long, flowing dustcoat like the concierge at the entrance gate and wearing the same type of cloth skull cap. This person breathed in the evening air for a moment and then stood aside, allowing a single file of about twenty people to pass by; they were dressed in a strange assortment of cast-off clothing.

Once out in the open air, this procession broke up. Like monks meditating in a cloister, some stood pensively in the middle of the terrace in front of the house; others, plunged in solitary thought, began to walk up and down the main path, every man alone, some staring at the ground, some gazing at the stars. The strange brotherhood slowly dispersed through the park; two of its members passed in front of Napoleon without seeing him, but in the shadows Napoleon himself began to tremble violently as he recognized their clothing at last. The key to the mystery came to him in a flash—and this normally fearless man felt himself for a moment transfixed with terror. Was it really possible that the medical officer had planned to trap him like this? Was he really capable of such a dreadful scheme?

One of the walkers came and sat on the same bench as Napoleon but did not look at him. Like his companions, he was wearing some sort of shabby fancy dress, improvised from bits and pieces, a patched-up mixture of cheap finery and rags which attempted to reproduce the classical dress of Napoleon in the field, as it was always pictured in the popular imagination: gray frock coat, white waistcoat and trousers, *grand cordon* around his neck, riding boots; a wooden sword completed the outfit. As for the famous little hat, it was made of thick paper, fairly carefully sewn and stuck together, and daubed with India ink.

Napoleon stared at him, hypnotized: under the grotesque disguise, a frightful thing to behold, the pale face bore the stamp of pensive nobility; the thin lips indicated inflexible resolve; under the paper hat, the staring eyes, accentuated by a drooping lock of hair, probed the depths of the night. It was as if, through the years, the relentless effort of thought—or rather of the single obsession that had taken the place of bygone thoughts—had succeeded in slowly modifying the features of his physical exterior to make it conform to the strict likeness of the Emperor. This miserable wreck presented an image of his model a thousand times more faithful, more worthy, and more convincing than the unlikely bald fruiterer who, seated beside him, was examining him with such amazement.

Other napoleons came and went around him; in the middle of the lawn, where a patch of white mist now hovered, one of them peered into the shadows through a cardboard telescope; another spread an old newspaper on the stone balustrade, as if it were a staff map. There were some who sat astride rusty garden chairs, lost in thought. And despite the forlorn parade of their borrowed garb, despite even the incongruous movements and bizarre postures— there was one of the company who only moved about by hopping, following the complicated layout of an imaginary game of hopscotch, and there was a short fat man who spun around on his heel like a top, with arms outstretched and coattails flying in the wind—all their faces showed a kind of solemn melancholy, a pensive seriousness, which was oddly impressive.

A bell rang. Like schoolboys at the end of recess, they formed ranks and filed back to the house, where one of the ubiquitous guards in a greatcoat was waiting for them under the lamp on the terrace.

Napoleon clenched his teeth and crouched in the shadow of the elm. He waited for a long while without moving.

Now indivisible from the darkness, the garden was once more silent and still.

He got up at last; his legs were stiff, his clothes were now quite damp.

Turning his back to the house, he crept along the lawn under the cover of the tall trees, then took the path in the direction from which he had come.

His eyes were now accustomed to the dark. From time to time he stopped for a moment to listen; but each time, all he could hear was the slight sound of the wind stirring the leaves.

At last the entrance gate came into view. When he saw the patch of light which the streetlamp cast on the high pillars of the gate, he felt like the sailor who, in the depths of the night, suddenly catches sight of the first light on the shore.

Slowly, silently, he drew near to the little door. He felt for the bolt: it had been padlocked!

He looked up. From the inside, the surface of the gate was nothing but smooth, slightly shiny sheet metal, surmounted by iron spikes which pointed at the stars.

To both left and right, the high walls bristling with pieces of broken glass made climbing impossible.

Twenty paces away, there stood a little gate-keeper's lodge, half submerged under wistaria; its only window was dimly lit by the glow of a candle.

He made up his mind immediately—and anyway, he had no choice. No longer trying to muffle the sound of his footsteps, and feigning confidence, he walked straight toward the lodge and banged on the window. He had already made up his story, which he would tell quite coolly: he had come to discuss food supplies with the director of the institution, Dr. Quinton. The name of this alienist, in charge of a mental hospital in the suburbs, had just come to his mind in a flash; though he had never met him personally, he had often heard the medical officer mention him as an old schoolmate and frequent partner at billiards. Napoleon's prodigious memory had registered and stored this bit of information months ago, and now his sudden predicament instantly triggered the connection.

. . . But he did not even have to tell his tale; no doubt, his face and appearance were enough to suggest the healthy vulgarity of a trades-man—or had the concierge received specific instructions?—the fact remains that the latter scarcely glanced at him as he shuffled sleepily out of his lodge and, without showing the least curiosity, unbolted the little door and with com-plete indifference returned him to the indiffer-ence of the world outside.

AS THE GATE SHUT behind him, he found himself back in the empty street, under a street-lamp where moths flew round and round in the light.

He had some difficulty working out where he was in this unfamiliar part of town. He tried different streets and got lost. When at last he arrived in the neighborhood of the Impasse-des-Chevaliers-du-Temple, it was nearly midnight.

Before going home, he was stubbornly determined to call in at Les Trois Boules again. Too late! He was told that the medical officer had come back that evening but had left again almost immediately with his belongings, and that he had left no address.

Napoleon was never to see him again. He made some inquiries in the days that followed, but his heart was not in it. Actually, he was no longer so anxious to lay hands on the deserter again. If he had wanted to, he could probably have found a lead from Dr. Quinton, but he found the very idea of meeting this person and revisiting the scene of his recent ordeal unspeakably repugnant.

As for the Ostrich, she was even less enthusiastic about seeing her former boarder again. His departure had brought her a sudden feeling of relief. The goodhearted soul could never have deliberately done anything to get rid of him, but now that he had left, it seemed that nothing could stand in the way of the new life that she saw opening up ahead of her—a calm life, a far cry from the stormy existence through which her heroic husband and his friends had dragged her for so many years—an ordinary life perhaps, but one that could finally bring her something like happiness.

She felt an ever-increasing admiration and affection for the man she always called Eugène.

Perhaps she was vaguely worried by a certain aloofness, a certain moodiness that her companion could not manage to suppress—although this mystifying aspect of his character played some part in the very respect and blind faith that she had come to feel toward him.

One deep desire obsessed her—it was the hidden thorn in her side. She dreamed of being able to legalize their union. She tried to reason with herself, and tell herself time and time again that the tranquil intimacy of their life together had no real need to be sanctioned by a mayor, but to no avail. In spite of everything, it seemed to her that without this official ceremony something would always be missing, the one thing perhaps that would have allowed her to know that happiness she secretly longed for. However, she would never have dared confess it to him openly; in spite of everything, he still made her feel a shyness she could not overcome. Perhaps one day he would, of his own accord, make the suggestion she wished so much to hear. Perhaps it was just a question of time; perhaps she just had to wait patiently. Perhaps . . . She cherished this hope, while sensing that there were some secret obstacles the exact nature of which she could not fathom.

At an auction sale she bought a huge Empire-style mahogany bed, with brass mounts in the shape of sphinxes, that had belonged to a bankrupt solicitor. It was a real extravagance—in spite of the upturn in business under Napoleon's forceful and imaginative direction, their capital was still relatively modest—but failing the ceremony she longed for, this majestic piece of furniture did at least seem to confer some sort of semiofficial ratification on their union.

So, from that day on, they slept together in the big bed. But they dreamed different dreams.

WHILE HE APPRECIATED the Ostrich's devotion, Napoleon was worried by the new turn his situation seemed to be taking.

His indomitable will, which the worst misfortunes could not have shaken, had imperceptibly been diverted toward domestic joys and small-time prosperity. This unexpected success, trifling though it was, nevertheless brought with it a kind of ease which he could not entirely ignore. It was beginning to transform the ground beneath his feet into a soft, shifting terrain where his resolution could become weak and slowly sink without trace. The more business improved and the Ostrich filled his life with touching new comforts, the less he resembled the real Napoleon.

Every time he went to the barber's, he stared into the double mirror and was horrified yet fascinated to see how his original features were disappearing little by little and being replaced by those of a stranger he despised and hated, and who inspired in him a growing feeling of disgust. He had put on a lot of weight and was now completely bald. If he had looked like this when he met Bommel (Justin), how could the sergeant ever have recognized him? And—not so long ago—the medical officer himself? When, after finalizing a particularly clever deal, he heard himself being congratulated by some broker in colonial goods who paid tribute to his brilliant business acumen, a burning lust for action ran through him—oh! to start again from scratch, to break free at once from this warm morass that threatened to engulf him!

Yet the medical officer's prophetic jibe, advising him to be content with making his fortune in watermelons, still rang in his ears, and the memory of that twilight visit to Dr. Quinton's asylum hung over him like an imminent threat. Besides, this threat was quite real, as he was soon to find out.

He had made a tentative attempt—rather an awkward one, it is true—to get the Ostrich to share in his secret.

The result of this approach was disastrous. At first, she did not understand anything; then, when she finally made out what he seemed to be aiming at, a heartrending look of astonishment and terror spread over her face. Napoleon realized how distressed she was and did his best to beat a retreat, making a laborious effort to change the subject of their conversation. She pretended to follow what he was saying, fighting hard not to burst into tears.

During the days that followed, she was careful not to mention the incident, but she secretly watched him all the time. She tended him with anxious concern, as if he were a convalescent getting over a serious illness; she begged him to look after himself, forbade him to stay up late; she lovingly prepared nourishing broths, and made him swallow potions. She was forever putting her hand on his forehead, pretending it was a caress, so that she could take his temperature.

Napoleon feigned not to notice, but he was perfectly well aware of the panic that his rash move had caused. The Ostrich's reaction had filled him with utter dismay, and he now realized that a lot of preparatory work would have to be done before she was able to accept the truth.

First he waited until the unfortunate effect of his first approach had somewhat abated.

When the Ostrich seemed to have almost forgotten the incident, and to a certain extent recovered her former equanimity, he thought he could risk trying again. But this time, in spite of all his caution and tact, the result was even more disastrous: he had scarcely brought up the subject, when she burst into tears, and became so dreadfully agitated that he vowed never to venture into this territory again. But in the meantime, he had to find a way to calm her down—which he did in a rather clumsy fashion. First he tried to pass off the whole story as a bad joke, then he contradicted himself by admitting to whims and fantasies which came, he was sure, from his digestive problems.

However, these confused explanations did no good at all; he could not manage to calm her. She caught him at his own game and begged him to see a doctor. She said she knew an excellent stomach specialist. Napoleon made some vague promises, while firmly resolving to avoid any such consultation. But this time he would not get out of it so easily!

One day when he came home a little earlier than usual, he surprised the Ostrich deep in conversation with an unknown visitor.

When she saw him, the Ostrich jumped to her feet, in a great state of confusion. The stranger, on the other hand—a short man, bent and cold as a cucumber, and tightly buttoned up to his chin in a brown overcoat—remained unruffled and merely stared at Napoleon with a kind of professional detachment. The Ostrich launched into voluble introductions: ". . . an old friend . . . a former comrade of the late Truchaut . . . just passing through . . . came in by chance . . . stayed to lunch . . . pleasure to see each other again . . . to meet . . . what's more an excellent doctor, in fact a stomach specialist, DR. QUINTON! . . ."

Had the visitor noticed the start that Napoleon had not been able to suppress when he heard his name? The doctor kept looking at him; his eyelids were strangely bereft of lashes, giving his eyes an unpleasantly fixed stare.

Napoleon made a superhuman effort to control the fury that was boiling inside him, and to act naturally as he moved about under the gaze of this disturbing, solemn, frog-like creature. First he tried fulsome politeness, but the exaggerated suavity of his words sounded so false that he himself was immediately alarmed by it. He felt trapped: whatever he did now, everything would be evidence against him; an angry outburst would certainly be the end of him; but on the other hand, hypocritical urbanity and the calculated weighing of words, far from allaying suspicion, would only tend to justify an even more alarming diagnosis. Finding himself in an extremely perilous situation, he finally chose the tactic that would give least away: burying his hands in his waistcoat to hide their trembling, he lapsed into an apathetic silence.

Quinton, who was no less taciturn, continued observing him with an air of morose satisfaction.

The Ostrich kept moving aimlessly around them, rummaging about among the pots and pans, shifting chairs from one place to another.

The ordeal seemed to last forever; they had to drink an aperitif, eat a meal, have coffee, sip liqueurs, smoke a cigar.

And still the silence continued.

Napoleon felt dizzy, he began seeing things. Instead of the brown overcoat opposite him, he sometimes thought he saw a long dustcoat and a cloth skull cap; and from the food the Ostrich had prepared, delicious though it was, there suddenly rose the stale refectory odor that he had smelled one evening deep inside a walled garden. It made him feel sick. He forced himself to take a copious second helping to overcome the feeling, but it was such a struggle to keep control of himself that, although his eating habits were normally very frugal and discreet, he suddenly began to devour his food in the most repulsive manner, chewing like a hyena. The Ostrich, who was astonished and appalled by this noisy, messy feeding frenzy, was by now close to tears. As for Quinton, he observed his subject shrewdly, nodding his head with the knowing expression of an expert.

AFTER QUINTON LEFT, Napoleon made a dreadful scene. He could almost have beaten the Ostrich. He smashed a china coffeepot and two vases. The Ostrich wept floods of tears. Moans arose here and there from children crouched in corners. Everyone was frightfully unhappy; they seemed to feel that it was the end of an era that would never return.

In the days and weeks that followed, they nonetheless tried to go on with their lives as though nothing had happened. The Ostrich swore to him that she would never, never again take it upon herself to call a doctor. And Napoleon, for his part, resolved once more never to try to include the poor woman in a secret that was obviously too much for her to cope with. No further word about the whole affair was exchanged between them, and on the surface their life went on as before—but only on the surface. Previously, during the long hours they spent alone together in the evenings, silence had wrapped them round in a warm feeling of security, whereas now it became unbearable, loaded with permanent menace.

The Ostrich watched over him incessantly with pathetic tender concern, and whenever he suddenly raised his head and saw the anxious questioning of that gaze which was always upon him, she turned her head away with a start, trying to hold back the tears that were always on the point of overflowing.

Silence frightened her, but she was even more afraid when he did occasionally speak. She always feared the threat of some double meaning behind the most banal expressions, and lived in dread of suddenly discovering in the most harmless remarks that the nightmare was lying in wait and ready to return.

The poor woman zealously did her best to keep up the pretense of a calm, happy life; then suddenly she would have to escape to the kitchen and cry until she could cry no more.

This make-believe was no less trying for Napoleon. In spite of all the pity he felt for her, he was quite lucid in his assessment of the dreadful danger he was in because of that innocent creature. And so, although it would grieve him to have to do it, he now had to consider breaking an attachment that could prove disastrous for him. Obviously, of all the strange ordeals that had crossed the path of his return to power, this separation would be by no means the least painful, but he could certainly draw many lessons from it which would be of benefit to him in the future.

He began to perceive more clearly that greatness should always be on its guard against the snares of happiness. The most brilliant achievements of his past career had been but a dream from which he was awakening at last. It was only *now* that his genius was coming to maturity. The epic of his past was no more than a confused and aimless burst of youthful energy compared with what he would be able to achieve, now that there would be no emotions, no attachments to stand between his creative intelligence and his will to act. He was reaching a higher plane of existence, and on these heights he breathed deeply of an air so pure that it would have burned the lungs of ordinary men.

From that moment on, victory seemed assured. It was only a matter of organization. He therefore coldly and methodically once more set about drawing up his plans.

First of all, he had to forge his weapons. He began by compiling a series of dossiers on the leading ministers, high bureaucrats, and military personnel who had served under the Empire and who had succeeded in gaining a position of influence in the present regime. It should be possible, if not by appealing to their loyalty, at least by having recourse to blackmail—and that was an essential part of these dossiers, based on his prodigious memory and on his knowledge of the political, civil, and criminal affairs of the Empire—progressively to persuade a certain number of these authorities to put secretly at his disposal forces that they already partially controlled in ministries, the government services, the Chamber of Deputies, the Senate, and, above all, in the army and the police. In that way, a clandestine power would grow little by little within the official power structure, replicating its functions and sapping its energies, until the day when, sure of its hidden network, with one stroke the former could take over from the latter, which would now be obsolete.

The organization chart of this secret power structure was beginning to take shape on paper, but its theoretical development still needed considerable research. He often had to go to libraries, where he sometimes spent whole afternoons consulting newspapers from the time of the Empire, old collections of the *Moniteur*, and a variety of other archival material.

However, this meant that he neglected the business, which began to suffer. The Ostrich became more and more alarmed about it, but dared not say anything. Napoleon now went out in the evenings more often than not. As it was impossible to work on his dossiers when the Ostrich was there, he installed himself in some café, and there, sitting next to pensioners playing dominoes, he patiently continued planning the huge insidious process which would soon undermine the whole of France.

He came home very late at night. The Ostrich waited for him, keeping one of the innumerable fortifying foods, of which she alone had the secret, on the corner of the stove: chicken livers marinated in port, braised pigs' brains with chestnuts, steamed cod roe, etc.

This took up several hours of her day, and had become a sort of release for her anxiety.

A whole summer went by in this manner. Autumn came. Napoleon's work progressed steadily. His business came closer and closer to collapsing. Soon the moment would come for him to fly off again. He was sincerely sorry when he thought of the pain that his departure would cause the Ostrich, and he regretted not being able to leave the business in a healthier state. But what could he do? Sometime in the future a day would come when he could offer her a fair and honorable reward for her devotion.

AT THE BEGINNING of winter, the weather, which had been exceptionally fine up till then, suddenly deteriorated.

One evening, as Napoleon was walking home from a café where he had spent a long study session, he was caught in a sudden downpour. He arrived home soaked to the skin and numb with cold. The Ostrich put him to bed with a toddy and a hot-water bottle.

At about one o'clock in the morning, his tossing and turning woke her up; he was burning with fever and delirious. Panic-stricken, she roused the oldest of the children and sent him to fetch a local doctor.

The doctor finally arrived, just before dawn. He found the disheveled Ostrich running up and down stairs, putting pots and pans on the stove, making hot drinks, trying to control her fear with frantic activity. Napoleon lay with his eyes wide open, mumbling incoherently. The doctor was an old man who, having had a great deal of experience, had long ago lost faith in medicine. He diagnosed a galloping lung infection. He left complicated instructions for making a poultice, so that the Ostrich would have something to do. He promised to come back regularly in the days that followed.

He kept his promise. At every visit, he merely came into the bedroom for a moment, looked at the patient, who was still delirious, nodded his head thoughtfully without speaking, fumbled about among ironmongery in the bottom of his leather bag, took out one of two small bottles, handed over pills of various colors to the Ostrich, and, to keep her amused for a moment, taught her a new variation on the poultice recipe.

For five days and five nights, Napoleon's fever continued unabated. His naturally delicate constitution, weakened by what he had already gone through, could not fight this terrible fire.

On the morning of the sixth day, his temperature dropped and he regained consciousness for a moment. The Ostrich's hopes soared, but the doctor who had arrived on his daily visit immediately disillusioned her. Like the flames of a forest fire that die down only when everything has been reduced to ashes, the illness had wrought its havoc and now had nothing more to feed on.

. . . And so he is lucid again, but only enough to realize the extent of his weakness. He finds himself in the big mahogany bed, placed in the position that the doctor had recommended to the Ostrich, half sitting, propped up against a pile of pillows to prevent his throat being blocked. He is aware of the brightness of daylight through his closed eyelids and the weave of the sheet under his still fingers.

He would like to open his eyes; he has been

planning it for quite a while, like someone getting ready for a journey, for it is a huge effort which requires a great work of preparation throughout his pitifully weak body. To this end, he calls on what scattered reserves of energy he can still muster.

He has succeeded, he has managed to open his eyes for an instant. And now, diving down again behind his eyelids, which have closed once more, he sinks with his booty: in his mind, he goes over what he has just been able to snatch from the bright world of the living: the table in front of the window and on the table the open dossiers he had brought home on that last evening when he had returned home through the cold and rainy night. He is not cold anymore. Perhaps today there is even a little sunshine. Is it sunny today? But now he brings his thoughts back to the table. The Ostrich is sitting at the table, with her back toward him.

The shadows deepen over his eyelids. He feels a desperate need to tear himself free from the depths that are slowly sucking him down, and to rise to the surface once more.

He has had to make a brutal effort to open his eyes this second time, and again, the scrap of light he can only dimly make out is immediately snatched away from him. And while he is sinking down once more, through the distant roar from the depths that starts humming again in his ears, he can still hear, with crystalline clarity, the Ostrich as she cries softly, like the murmuring of a spring, and then from time to time the sound of a page being turned.

Like a diver in the gloom of the deep, he feels an urgent need to come up for air, but in his exhaustion he can no longer battle against the current that carries him ever faster, ever farther from the daylight. He struggles and tires himself out with superhuman efforts, the fever returns, and he topples into the abyss. The Ostrich rushes to his bedside. He can see nothing, but clings to her hand.

He clings, and yet keeps plunging down, spinning around in a great whirl of fleeting lights and images.

And then suddenly, as his thoughts flee in chaos, an agonizing revelation pierces his mind: he has just been informed that if he wants to pass through to THE OTHER SIDE, he will have to undergo a test, and he will be asked one question only: What is the Ostrich's first name?

Terror-stricken, he realizes in a blinding flash that he has forgotten, that he does not know, that HE HAS NEVER KNOWN THE OSTRICH'S FIRST NAME! A spasm shakes his entire body, he arches his back against the bed, he struggles, he makes wild, desperate efforts—quickly, quickly, do anything to find her name, it's the last chance—if he cannot fill this dreadful yawning gap in his soul before he has to appear in front of Them, his ship will be turned away from port forever, sent to the north; they will put him off at Copenhagen, where he will lead a flock of penguins on desolate icefields, exiled for all time with no hope of return. He chokes, his throat rattles, his body jerks uncontrollably, his teeth chatter.

There is a cool hand on his forehead. The Ostrich bends over him with infinite tenderness. His tense, knotted brain relaxes a little and his tongue loosens: ". . . Name? . . . Name? . . ."

He is appalled to hear himself saying at last, "What is MY name?" but it is too late to try again. Where would he find the strength to correct his mistake, to rephrase it, to link the heavy words together one after the other like a train, what-is-your-name, and send the convoy off again toward the light that has now vanished?

The Ostrich bends down to his pillow and whispers, "Eugène, your name is Eugène . . ." When he hears these words he gives a sudden desperate start, which she misinterprets, for she immediately adds even more softly and closer to his ear, as if it were a secret, "Napoleon, you are my Napoleon." The sweetness of these last words cuts him to the heart, it is the finish, he falls backwards. As he sinks even farther, he is still holding her hand, and for a moment longer he can feel her cool soft hand in his. Then soon this last link slips from his grasp.

After whirling down through dull blue-green depths, at last he begins to fall more slowly, and now he is floating, almost still. The night is nearly over and a gray dawn is breaking beneath his eyelids. Far away, and muffled by distance, drums are rolling and fifes are playing their shrill notes. The regiments are marching to the front line; the din of men and stamping horses increases. The sound of the fifes is as sharp as early-morning air—and all the while, those drums keep beating. From time to time, quite close, can be heard the snorting of a restive horse, the tinkling of a harness, brief commands reverberating over the serried ranks.

And now a huge red sun emerges out of the mist, the sun that shines on victory mornings. It rises in the sky, a sky bright with rainbow-colored clouds.

How vast the plain is! It is vaster than all the plains on earth, pale and shifting; it is the boundless sea, the sea without memory! And with his arm extended in a broad sweeping gesture, pointing to the day-star as it rises, Nigger-Nicholas exults in his innocent triumph.